BREAKAWAY RECOVERY

BREAKAWAY RECOVERY

HOW TO CRUSH YOUR ADDICTIONS, MASTER YOUR EMOTIONS, AND LIVE YOUR BEST LIFE

TOM JORDAN

reframebuddha@gmail.com

ISBN: 979-8-9899779-0-1 (paperback)
ISBN: 979-8-9899779-1-8 (ebook)

Ordering Information:
Special discounts are available on quantity purchases by corporations, associations, and others. For details, contact reframebuddha@gmail.com

Dedication

To the victims of addiction and their families and communities and to those working in the field of addiction treatment for your tireless efforts to free those being controlled by the scourge of addiction.

To the Spectrum Deadly Dogs, those among my many clients who were willing to go the extra mile to get and remain drug free. Your determination, grit, and hard work has never ceased to amaze and inspire me. Working with you over all these many years has made me a better person. You've helped me more than you will ever know.

TABLE OF CONTENTS

INTRODUCTION

Giving up smoking is the easiest thing in the world.
I know because I've done it thousands of times.
—Mark Twain, author

It's 1966, and I'm with my friends David and Jamie, smoking cigarettes on a hill overlooking the country club in Burlington, Massachusetts, and waiting for it to get dark out. We're planning to break into the main building of the club, where David is sure we'll find a case of beer. Although I'm 13 years old and eager to drink alcohol for the first time, I'm not too keen on breaking and entering, so I'll stay back as the lookout. If I see the cops or any cars enter the parking lot, I'm to hoot like an owl. I kid you not. That's the plan—a sure sign we're a pack of criminal masterminds.

It finally gets dark, and my friends head for the building.

I wait for what seems like an eternity before I finally hear them making their way back up the hill. I can see David is carrying something. It's the coveted case of Schlitz beer. We're all ecstatic at the thought of drinking and getting drunk for the first time.

This will prove to be a transformational experience.

I grab the little ring on the top of the can and pull. To this day, I can still hear its pop and the fizz. I hold the can up to my mouth and start guzzling, pouring beer into my mouth and down my throat as fast as I can. I manage to get about half the can down and stop for a breather. When I do, I notice something: I am not the same person anymore. I'm no longer Tom

Jordan, the anxious teenager with low self-esteem. I'm transformed into … Elvis Presley, the king of rock and roll! I'm suddenly on top of the world.

With that one drink, I felt as if I'd become the desire of every girl and the envy of every boy. It's amazing what half a can of beer can do for a 13-year-old boy.

My new identity as one of the "cool kids" in town would take me to places I couldn't imagine—some of them thrilling, like a Jimi Hendrix concert. Other adventures would be less exciting and more troublesome. The reality is, living like Elvis Presley isn't sustainable if you're not Elvis Presley, or even if you are. We all know what addiction did to him. If you're reading this book, you also know what addiction has done to you. The information here will empower you to address those troublesome outcomes and put you on a completely new path, as it has for me and the clients I've worked with over these many years as an addiction specialist.

Breakaway Recovery, the program detailed in this book, is the result of what I've learned over the past 50 years, first by eliminating dozens of my own vices and then from working with hundreds of clients as a detox counselor, residential counselor, outpatient counselor, methadone clinic counselor, clinical supervisor, clinical director, and manager of a program, where I played a pivotal role in developing and implementing agency-wide addiction treatment philosophies and best practices.

I've been on both sides of addiction, so I understand what you're going through, and I have the knowledge and the tools to help you on your journey. My goal is to share the strategies and tools I've acquired and developed over the course of my own recovery and my work as an addiction specialist. I trust you'll find the instructions detailed in this book to be of significant benefit.

What This Book Is About

This is a book about addiction, but even more to the point, it's about the suffering that comes with addiction and how we can put an end to both.

Addiction often comes on the heels of an epiphany. We take that first drink, for example, and our social anxiety instantly vanishes. After years of being wallflowers, we suddenly possess the power to become the life of the party, or Elvis, as was the case with me. Drinking alcohol, we discover, is the key to social confidence and popularity! Yet the vice we've relied on to boost our social confidence gradually reverses itself. What previously made us popular now rescinds that popularity, turning us into a social outcast, a pariah of sorts. Our former companions now want nothing to do with us. At best, they pity us. At worst, they despise us.

Whatever your vices may be, major or minor, you picked up this book because you've noticed or are beginning to notice that there's something not quite right about them. You may not be mainlining heroin but simply spending too much time looking at your smartphone. You have habits that, on some level, cause you problems. Still, despite their unwanted side effects, you've been unable to stop indulging in your addictive behaviors, and you don't know why.

That's the mystery this book sets out to solve: why do we continue to engage in behaviors that work against our own best interests?

At some point, your answer to that question will leap off the page and stare you squarely in the face. You'll be incapable of missing it, ignoring it, or denying it. And you'll hear that message in a way that is undeniably relevant to you and your situation. You'll have no choice but to recognize it for what it is. Still, this is only the beginning, albeit the most important beginning since your birth. Whenever this idea shows up, whether it's on the first page of this book or the last, pause for a moment and take it in. Revel in it. You have just experienced one of the most—if not the most—important turning points of your life.

This is a book about addiction: what it is, how it controls you, and how to overcome its potential-draining domination. It's also a book about how once you overcome addiction, you replace it. Using my breakaway recovery method, you'll learn how to identify, eliminate, and replace every last one of your addictive behaviors, vices, and bad habits.

Sound too good to be true? Keep reading.

Who This Book Is For

This is a book for people who routinely overdo it, who don't know when to quit, who can't seem to get enough, and who never know when enough is enough. It's for people who don't know that enough can be enough or don't understand the meaning of "too much." It's for the three-pack-a-day smokers, blackout drinkers, and hard-core junkies. It's for the party-till-you-puke crowd and weekend warriors who seldom wait for the weekend to start partying. It's for people who smoke too much, drink too much, eat too much, or shop too much. This is a book for hard-core hedonists who need hard-core recovery. It's for those of us who believe that anything worth doing is worth overdoing—but haven't figured out what's worth doing.

You may wish to eliminate only one vice. Let's assume for a moment that your goal in reading this book is simply to quit drinking alcohol. You're not interested in becoming vice-free. You're not interested in giving up your many other addictions. You'll be happy just to quit drinking. If that's the case, you won't need every idea that you'll find in this book. Not all the hundreds of clients I've helped quit drinking over the years needed every suggestion to get and stay sober. For some of you, a few ideas in this book—maybe even just one—could do the job.

That's right. It's possible that just one key concept will lead you to your goal of sobriety. Somewhere in the pages that follow, you'll find it. And it's possible that one is all it will take. The reason you drink and why you'll be better off without it will hit you in a way that you no longer feel the need to drink. True, you'll continue to indulge in other, perhaps less detrimental vices, but you will be free from your alcohol addiction or whatever your primary vice happens to be.

But this book is not intended only for those with a single vice they want to eliminate. It's also for those who have a long list of vices they want to discard. In other words, this is a book for serious quitters—people who intend to eliminate every vice that stands in the way of their success and happiness. Quitting, by which I mean eliminating your vices, is just the beginning. It's the start of something important and transformational that will not only replace your vices but do it in a way that catapults you to another level, one teeming with opportunities and possibilities.

This approach to recovery is for those of us who love to overdo it but don't love the unwelcome but inevitable side effects and high price of addiction. The blackouts, the hangovers, the overdoses, the DUIs, the lost jobs, and all the rest have taken their toll. I know—I've been there. Indulging may still have its moments. But the aftermath of those moments has become indefensible.

Most importantly, it's for people who are struggling with addictions but want more from themselves and their lives, who want to discover or successfully pursue their purpose, a purpose that is being hidden and hindered by their addictive behaviors. They have a hunger and a thirst that drives them to act addictively, and they long to direct their addictive urges and cravings to something that matters.

Is that you? Is there something you want to accomplish? Or is there a certain kind of person you want to become? If so, then this book was written for you. It's also written for those of you who aren't quite sure what you want. You just know you want something more than you've been settling for. That's okay. You don't have to know what it is. It's there inside you waiting to be discovered, and I'm here to help you discover it.

This book is for those who want more from life—certainly more than being trapped in the psychological cage called addiction. Let me warn you: it's not for the faint of heart, but neither is the addiction-filled life you've been living.

What You Can Expect

I can tell you from my own experience, and that of the many clients I have counseled over the years, that breaking free from addictive behaviors is not only possible, but it's also something at which you can excel—once you get the hang of it, that is. But don't let me mislead you. Addictions can be remarkably stubborn and can sometimes seem nearly impossible to break. What does it take? First, you must understand addiction, what it is and what causes it. Once you understand what addiction is, you must understand what causes *you* to become addicted. Only by understanding the nature of addiction and its cause can you begin the work necessary to put an end to it.

Unfortunately, current treatment strategies are largely ineffective because most aren't based on a sound, evidence-based theory of addiction and its cause. But when you use a strategy that addresses this, giving up addictive behaviors becomes possible. On the other hand, if your strategy is based on a misunderstanding about addictive behavior and fails to address its cause, your attempts to stop indulging will become wearisome and exasperating. Addiction treatment is often a revolving door, with many people going in and out of 12-step programs, detoxes, and residential treatment for years—or even decades—yet still not getting clean or sober.

If you have already tried traditional recovery methods and found them wanting, reading this book will give you another option, one that can work for you. As you read, your view of your addictive behavior will start to shift. You'll learn to see your addiction for what it is—a failed and often tragic attempt to find happiness where no happiness exists. You'll start to see that you, while not solely responsible for your addictive behaviors, are responsible for giving them up, and you'll start to learn concrete strategies and techniques for identifying and eliminating the cause. As you begin to practice and apply these techniques to your addictive thoughts, feelings, fantasies, and behaviors, you'll notice that the grip of your addictive impulses begins to loosen. Your desire to indulge in your addictive behaviors will gradually lose its strength until you finally have no desire left.

That's right. Your addictive behaviors will eventually lose their appeal altogether. It turns out this is how all of us overcome our addictions, whether we realize it or not. We gain reliable insights into our addictive behavior and its consequences through painful experiences or by using our reason and imagination to see into the true nature of our circumstances.

This new view allows us to lose interest in what was once an irresistible obsession to indulge.

This book will show you how to reframe your triggers, using your reasoning, intelligence, and imagination so you won't have to learn the hard way, as so many others do. And when the glorious moment of final liberation arrives, you'll feel both relieved and delighted. You'll have no sense of loss or deprivation. You won't have to grieve the loss of your "best friend," as you may have been instructed to do in other programs. You'll experience no sense of loss or deprivation because you'll have seen the truth of your addictive behavior: it is your worst enemy, not your best friend.

Nor will the process always be stressful or unpleasant, although you will have your moments, of course. With practice, eliminating your addictions will become something you enjoy working toward and ultimately accomplishing. Once you break free from a particular addictive behavior, you'll find yourself looking forward to the challenge of disregarding the next one. Nor will you view it as giving something up. Instead, you'll have learned to see the addictive behavior for what it is—something you're happy to be rid of.

You'll come to realize that living without an addictive behavior is like walking without a thorn in your side or pebble in your shoe. You'll feel relieved that it's gone. The pain that comes with addiction will be replaced with the exhilaration of freedom. And any benefits or pleasure you once derived from indulging will be generously compensated for in ways that will both surprise and delight you. And that's just part of the beauty of the method you'll take away from this book. You'll learn to frame your new-found abstinence as a gain, not a loss. And it will *feel* like a gain!

Ironically, the more extreme your addictive nature, the better you'll do in following the path laid out in this book. Until now, your purpose has been to pursue and indulge in a series of vices. Very soon, all that will change as you embark on a new purpose with your trademark passion. This book will show you how to harness and direct your addictive nature. You will finally put your energy to good use, using it to master your thoughts, emotions, and behaviors, while discovering your life's purpose, fulfilling your potential, and realizing your highest aspirations.

Obsession is only a bad thing when you're obsessed with the wrong thing. You'll learn to harness your propensity to overindulge, turning it to your advantage. What was once your mortal enemy will become your greatest ally.

How to Use This Book

Read this book once all the way through before taking the 10 steps or doing the related exercises. This will give you an understanding of how the program works, and that's important. Once you understand the concepts, read the book a second time. This time, follow the instructions for each of the 10 steps, which form the crux of the program, and do the other exercises.

Remember, to know and not to do is not to know. Insight alone is the booby prize. Be sure to do the work by following the instructions for each of the 10 steps and for all of the exercises you find throughout the book. Take as much time as you need.

Why All the Repetition?

As you make your way through this book, you'll notice I repeat a fair amount of information. This is deliberate. As humans, we learn through repetition. The more we rehearse an idea or a skill, the better we are able to put it to use. Many of you already know this if you've read other personal development books. Personally, I read books over and over until I not only understand what I've read but can actually apply it.

A Note on Language

In the following pages, I use the word "addiction," but the term for this affliction has evolved over the years. The American Psychiatric Association's *Diagnostic and Statistical Manual of Mental Disorders* (*DSM*) has called it different things at different times. For example, "substance abuse" is now "substance use disorder." Clients I've worked with often don't use this language and instead refer to themselves as alcoholics, drunks, dope fiends, or crackheads. They find using these terms is more to the point and encourages them to change. Others prefer not to use these terms. For example, some of my clients avoid Alcoholics Anonymous (AA) meetings because they'd rather not say, "Hi, my name is Tom, and I'm an alcoholic." Others find that helpful because it keeps their addiction up front.

To keep it real, I sometimes refer to those of us prone to addiction as addicts. True, no one is literally an addict. We are human beings who struggle with addictions. Still, it is part of what we do, so it's part of who we are. No one minds being referred to as a parent, sister, artist, or entrepreneur. But those are just one-dimensional labels, too, for raising children, having a sibling, creating art, or building businesses. It's just easier and more convenient to say, "I'm an artist," than to say, "I'm a person who creates art for a living." It's also easier and more convenient to say "alcoholic" than explaining that "I'm a person who drinks too much, sometimes to the point of blacking out, and can't stop, no matter how hard I try."

I also use the words "alcoholic," "addict," and even "junkie" and "crackhead" when referring to clients and former clients who refer to themselves that way and find it helpful in staying clean and sober. If you find those terms offensive, I get it. But not all of us do. I myself do not prefer those labels. Instead of using the terms "recovering" or "recovered alcoholic," I think of myself as someone who was once addicted to drinking alcohol and, thankfully, no longer is.

While "substance use disorder" may be the official term at the time of this writing, I won't be using it. I prefer to call a spade a spade. Addiction, in my opinion, best describes these behaviors. And there are often no substances involved in addiction. People get addicted to gambling, playing video games, and watching pornography. These are all potentially addictive behaviors. Drinking alcohol is one too. In that sense, all addictions are behavior addictions. For example, as we'll explore in more detail, we are not addicted to alcohol per se or the act of drinking alcohol. It's the way drinking alcohol makes us *feel* that gets us addicted. Whether you personally long to break out of an addictive rut or know someone who does, I trust you'll find what you're looking for in the pages that follow.

Let's begin.

2

ANATOMY OF AN EPIDEMIC

I can resist everything except temptation.

—Oscar Wilde, author

Like you, I've had my fair share of addictions: television, cigarettes, coffee, ice cream, and cake. Not to mention my personal favorites: sex, drugs, and rock 'n' roll, to name just a few. I indulged in these and many other addictive behaviors. Why? Because they made me feel good … until they didn't. They all started out on a high note, but in time, I began to view each one as a problem. Smoking cigarettes became a problem. Drinking beer became a problem. Frequenting bars and nightclubs became a problem. Chasing women became a problem. In my mid-20s, I realized that I depended on my addictive behaviors to make me feel good *and* that they were no longer doing that. In fact, they made me miserable. No matter how many cigarettes I smoked, how many beers I drank, or how many women I chased, I wasn't satiated. As they say in AA, "One is too many. A thousand is never enough."

I was the living embodiment of that principle. Consider this: At age 25, I quit drinking alcohol. Soon after, I went to the donut shop, ordered two large coffees with cream and extra sugar, guzzled the first cup, and sipped and enjoyed the second. When I was done with the second cup, I went back and ordered another two and repeated the process. For years, I continued this substitute addiction to keep myself high on caffeine and distracted from the often unforgiving nature of reality. I couldn't get enough.

But as we shall see, not being able to get enough isn't the problem. The problem is what we can't get enough *of.* That's the good news. You won't have to give up your lusty nature. I learned this liberating fact, along with other relevant insights, from studying Buddhism. Buddha himself, while known for renouncing worldly pleasures, has nonetheless been referred to as a pleasure junkie. The secret, as Buddha himself discovered, is not renouncing all pleasure. It's finding the *right kind* of pleasure. It's being able to enjoy pleasure *without becoming attached* to it and ultimately transcending it altogether. Transcending our *attachments* to unwholesome and even wholesome pleasures is the secret to becoming and remaining vice-free. How Buddha learned to live happily without the unwholesome pleasures—and how you can too—will be explained shortly. First, though, let's identify and define the problem: What is addiction?

In this chapter, we'll look at addiction from the perspective of the Four Noble Truths, the foundation of Buddhism. Using these Four Noble Truths, we'll reveal the mechanics of how addiction takes hold and how you can break free from its steely grip. These are the Four Noble Truths:

Life is laced with suffering.
Suffering is caused by craving and attachment.
There is an end to suffering.
There is a path that leads to the end of suffering.

As it turns out, addiction itself isn't the problem. Rather, addiction is an attempted solution to an underlying problem. We smoke cigarettes, drink wine, watch pornography, or engage in any number of other addictive behaviors to escape from that problem, the real problem, the only problem we ever face: the problem of suffering.

This book refers to addiction in the broadest sense, and we'll be looking at the full spectrum of addictive behaviors: bad habits, vices, dependencies, and attachments—even attachments we typically view as wholesome. You see, it's not just hard-core vices like heroin or crack or alcohol that count as addictions. It's also other less serious vices, like playing video games or hanging out on Facebook. It's also bad habits like biting your fingernails or procrastinating or eating sugary snacks. Then there's the habit of developing dependencies and forming unhealthy attachments to what should be good things in our lives: our careers, children, or health.

Alcoholism is also referred to as alcohol dependence because we come to depend on alcohol to relieve our anxiety, boredom, and other unpleasant emotions. Yet even depending on more wholesome pursuits like going for a run can be problematic when we become overly attached or dependent on them.

Everything in life is impermanent—the good, the bad, the beautiful, and the ugly. We become attached to and dependent on certain things to keep us happy. There's a better way. The goal of this book is to reduce the pursuits, activities, people, places, and things you depend too heavily on for your emotional well-being so you can become as independently happy as possible.

Now we'll take a closer look at Buddha's Four Noble Truths and how they relate to addiction.

The Problem

No one plans on becoming a drug addict, yet many born into drug-infested neighborhoods, for example, reluctantly concede that this will be their fate. But it's certainly not something they aspire to, not something they look forward to, and not something they intentionally commit to. No one sets out to be a drunk, a crackhead, or a dope fiend. We all imagine something better for ourselves, even those with little chance of attaining it. Some of us may even commit to something better, if only the vague idea of a better life.

But those vague aspirations and half-baked commitments soon fall by the wayside as our destructive behaviors take center stage in our lives.

Even if you're not addicted to drugs, not trading sex for money, or not eating out of a dumpster, chances are you're not doing as well as you could be. Maybe you have a job, but it's not a job you love or not a career. Or maybe it's a career you never chose or a career you chose based on incomplete or faulty information. You realize now that it was a bad choice. Yet you stay with it because it's convenient or familiar—not great, not particularly satisfying, and certainly not something you've always dreamed of doing. But hey, it could be worse. At least you have a job, right? And so, you distract yourself with texting or sexting or social media or smoking or drinking or playing the lottery, or all the above.

At least you're not a drug addict, right? Maybe you live in a nice neighborhood, not a drug-infested one, have a few good friends, go out to eat on weekends, and catch a movie or even a play now and then. Maybe you have a hobby you enjoy when you're not glued to the television set or the internet. Sure, you watch too much TV, spend more time on social media than you'd like, and drive yourself crazy reading and posting tweets. But, hey, you're not homeless, and you're not worried about where your next meal is coming from. True, there is that little problem with pornography, but it's not as if you're a rapist, right? (If you're watching pornography, however, you're supporting an industry that forces women and young girls into sex work.)

Now, let's look at what Buddha has to say about what's at the heart of the problem.

Suffering, Buddha's first noble truth and the problem at the heart of the issue this book addresses, goes by many names and comes in many forms, including:

- boredom,
- lethargy,
- apathy,
- loneliness,
- sadness,

- depression,
- misery,
- hopelessness,
- embarrassment,
- humiliation,
- hurt,
- guilt,
- regret,
- shame,
- envy,
- jealousy,
- irritation,
- annoyance,
- resentment,
- disgust,
- contempt,
- intolerance,
- anger,
- hatred,
- ill-will,
- agitation,
- stress,
- distress,
- anxiety,
- fear,
- dread,
- panic, and
- terror.

Each word on that list shares two things in common with all of the others. First, they represent a form of suffering. Second, each word denotes an emotion. Suffering, as we shall see, is always an emotional affair. We suffer not because of disappointments, not because of trouble or hardship, and not even because of tragedies, crises, or catastrophes. Nor is suffering solely the result of illness, injury, or pain. We suffer because of how we *feel* about these adversities—specifically, how we feel *emotionally*.

Adversity isn't the culprit. It's how we interpret and feel about it. Even physical pain isn't what makes us suffer. It's the emotions that come along with it. And those emotions arise not from the pain itself but from our interpretation of the pain and our reactions to it. If we interpret pain to mean that there's something wrong (that we've been hurt or injured), then suffering is sure to occur. If we interpret it to mean we're awesome because we just finished running our first marathon, then we don't experience suffering. We embrace our pain and feel proud of ourselves for enduring it. And yes, we can do the same with the pain associated with an injury or an illness.

Addiction is an attempt, albeit a poor one, to alleviate suffering. You drink because you hurt emotionally. You feel anxious, lonely, sad, or maybe just bored or restless. When you drink a six-pack of your favorite beer or watch your favorite TV show, those feelings recede. You feel relieved, and with the relief come feelings of pleasure. For a time, all is right with the world. That's what you wanted. It's what we all want, and it's all we want.

You may think you want something else: a new wardrobe, a day off from work, or a piece of cheesecake. But when we say we want a new car or a new house or a new partner, what we really want is the way we'll *feel* when we get the thing we desire and believe will make us happy. It's that feeling of happiness we want, not the new car. We're confused, and that's a shame because material things can't make us happy, at least not for long. And the happiness these things do temporarily bring is inferior to the happiness that comes with living a meaningful life, one with the right purpose and direction.

Breakaway Recovery will show you how to overcome suffering by living a good life or, as Buddha would say, by following the fourth noble truth. That starts with giving up your vices, the things you do to make yourself happy that aren't actually making you happy. In brief, you'll learn how to identify and eliminate your bad habits, your addictions, and your unhealthy attachments. As you eliminate those self-sabotaging behaviors, you'll replace them with empowering alternatives. As we'll see, this process is sometimes simple but not often easy. It can be summarized with two words: abandon and develop. Once you abandon a bad habit, you'll replace it by developing a new self-empowering alternative.

The Cause

In this section, we'll answer the question "What causes suffering?" Suffering, as we shall see, is the result of a complex set of causes and conditions. Let's look at the most prominent ones, one at a time.

Biology

From a strictly biological perspective, suffering starts with the body. We suffer because we have a body replete with pain receptors and a central nervous system that receives messages from those receptors. We experience those messages as unpleasant: sometimes mildly, sometimes moderately, sometimes highly unpleasant, and sometimes downright painful. And, as we all know and know all too well, pain hurts. To make matters worse, the part of our brain that registers physical pain also registers emotional pain. We have a brain that evolved to protect us by making things hurt, both physically and emotionally, and so we suffer. But we don't just suffer. We suffer deeply, and we suffer in multiple ways. And that's just from a biological perspective.

Natural Selection

From an evolutionary perspective, suffering starts with the brain, the brain that natural selection built. We suffer because our brains evolved with a narrow agenda: to stay alive so we can pass on our genes with the brain we inherited from our ancient ancestors. The brain's job was to look for trouble in a dangerous environment (that we modern humans no longer inhabit) by compulsively scanning the environment for threats to our survival—often finding threats where none exist.

In other words, our suffering arises from a brain equipped with an outdated, hypersensitive, and overreactive threat detector, among other less-than-optimal, outdated hardware, not to mention outdated software installed when we were young and impressionable. That software no longer serves the purpose it was originally meant to serve. Call it a less-than-perfect learning history. Combine natural selection with an early-childhood and adolescent learning history, and you get an organism primed for both addiction and suffering. Welcome to the human race.

As a species, then, we've inherited a brain designed to look for and find trouble, often where no trouble exists. When we discover our surroundings pose no threats, we look to the future, imagining what threats might await us there. It's called worrying, and we humans, because of our overprotective brains, do a lot of it. Even when we're safe from immediate physical threats such as famine, extreme weather conditions, wild beasts, and invading armies, our brains start scanning our social environments for fear we may have offended someone and so might be ostracized or exiled. Such a fate meant death for our ancestors, so our brains evolved to interpret even the slightest disapproval as potentially life threatening. We don't consciously see it that way, but our brain's fight-or-flight system does. And that's just our brain's hardware.

We also have faulty software, the individual learning histories I mentioned above, which is the way we were programmed as children to think and behave. For individual members of the human species, our brains were mostly wired from birth to age seven, then again during adolescence. Left unchecked, that less-than-optimal wiring follows us into adulthood and old age.

As a species, humans were also hardwired for splurging on sweet, salty, and fatty foods, which kept us alive as individuals. We were likewise hardwired for spreading our genes far and wide, which kept us alive as a species. Natural selection set us up to eat whatever food we could get our hands on and to procreate with as many partners as possible, which is not the best way to live, at least not in this day and age. And as if that's not bad enough, many of us grew up in the United States' quick fix culture, a culture that wired our brains for instant gratification. That's the kind of conditioning we got, some of us more than others, but all of us to one degree or another.

In short, we were born with self-seeking, self-gratifying, self-promoting brains, brains that then got wired for more of the same by the quick fix, capitalistic, consumer-based culture we grew up in. And we wonder why we struggle with addiction and why, despite our great good fortune, we experience so much needless suffering.

Note: As we shall see, it's not all bad. The brain is an amazing organ capable of being rewired, reprogrammed, and retrained. Yes, we can change and transcend our brain's hardware and software, but I'm getting ahead of myself—more on that later.

Chemistry

As we go about our lives, feelings provide important feedback. They keep us alive as individuals and as a species, telling us what to approach and what to avoid. That's why eating a banana and having sex both evolved to feel good. One keeps us going as individuals, the other as a species.

Feelings, then, are at the heart of our approach-avoidance system. They protect us from danger and death, but they can also get us into trouble because what feels good isn't always good for us and what feels bad isn't always bad for us. It's not a perfect system.

For example, being deprived of your favorite dessert feels bad. Your brain interprets it as a threat to your survival. While you don't consciously think of it that way, your brain does, so it floods your system with the hormone called cortisol. The cortisol surge feels bad enough to knock you off your diet because you know that eating the dessert will replace the bad feelings with good feelings. Although natural selection cares only about keeping us alive and reproducing, we care primarily about staying alive, not necessarily to reproduce but rather to enjoy ourselves.

Our goal is to avoid discomfort, pain, suffering, and unhappiness and to experience their opposites and enjoy ourselves. If we believe reproducing will make us happier, we'll do it. If not, we won't. We do whatever we imagine will make us happy, even though we may not always realize that's what we're doing—more on how that works coming up.

As I mentioned, your brain evolved to keep you alive. Its chief concern is your survival. Once it knows you're safe, it looks for reproduction opportunities. Stay alive and reproduce, that's what natural selection built you to do. Your brain uses a variety of neurochemicals to get you to comply. For example, when cortisol enters into the bloodstream, you experience it like a fire alarm going off in your brain. You sense that something's wrong, that there's a threat to your survival or well-being. It's an unpleasant feeling, and you instinctively act to remove it.

For example, you might feel hungry or thirsty. Hunger and thirst are unpleasant feelings that alert you to the need for food and water. Without them, you'll die. The more hungry or thirsty you get, the more cortisol your brain pumps into your bloodstream. The louder the alarm sounds, the more likely you are to respond. You experience this alarm as a form of suffering. The hungrier or the thirstier you feel, the louder the alarm gets. The louder the alarm rings, the more you suffer. The more you suffer, the more motivated you are to remove the suffering.

Other chemicals in your body—dopamine, serotonin, oxytocin, endo-cannabinoids, endorphins, and adrenaline—have the opposite effect. They alert you to opportunities and produce feelings that reward you for success. When they release into the bloodstream, you experience pleasure. You feel good. Dopamine produces the feeling of expectation, of good things to come. It puts you in pursuit of a goal. Serotonin produces the feeling of having attained status, of being respected or admired by others. Oxytocin produces the feeling of belonging to a group, of bonding with others. It's sometimes referred to as the cuddle chemical. Endocannabinoids bring on the feeling of satisfaction that comes with things like runner's high and being in the zone. Endorphins offer relief from pain. Adrenaline gets you feeling excited. It revs you up, preparing you to meet a challenge.[1]

What these chemicals all have in common is that they get us moving by making us feel one way or another. Unpleasant feelings get us moving away from something. Pleasant feelings get us moving toward something or returning to it. However, we get a fair share of false alarms in both directions. We often feel attracted to things that aren't in our best long-term interests. Likewise, we can feel aversion to things that are.

Natural selection wired us, using both pain and pleasure, to survive and reproduce. But the pain we experience does more than keep us alive. It also induces suffering. And the pleasure we experience often leads us to behavior that also results in suffering somewhere down the line. From an evolutionary perspective, we suffer because suffering helps to keep us alive and reproducing in a dangerous and competitive world—except, of course, when it doesn't.

Environment

From an environmental perspective, we suffer because we routinely encounter real or imagined adversities—people, places, events, or situations we deem to be threatening or dangerous. These are the triggers that get the ball of suffering rolling, from disappointments, failures, and rejection to isolation, illness, and death. We experience these adversities as unpleasant, unwelcome, and unacceptable intruders into our lives. We resent and resist them, so we suffer. As I pointed out earlier, it's not these adversities themselves that cause our suffering but our interpretations and reactions to them. Suffering, like happiness, is an inside job. No, not completely, not exclusively, but most importantly—most importantly because it's our interpretations and our reactions to adversity that we have the most control over, and so they are the greatest chance of reevaluating and redefining adversity in a way that works for instead of against us.

---

1   This description is based on the early, incomplete science of brain chemistry. Exactly which neurotransmitter does what isn't all that relevant for our discussion. We are interested in our subjective feelings—in other words, what's going on in our minds, not our brains. The specific chemicals involved aren't really the point.

Cognition

From a psychological perspective, then, we suffer because we entertain self-defeating thoughts about the adversities we encounter. We interpret what's happening in a way that makes us lustful, anxious, depressed, jealous, angry, and so on. These emotions make up the experience we call suffering. Suffering, as I've argued, is always an emotional affair. Adversities, although related to suffering, never directly cause our suffering. Our suffering comes from our emotional reactions to the thoughts we have about the adversities we encounter. First comes the adversity. Then comes our interpretation or thoughts. Then comes the suffering, always in the form of one or more of the toxic emotions.

Craving

Let's look at suffering from a purely Buddhist perspective. In his presentation of the Four Noble Truths, Buddha identified suffering as the first of those noble truths and craving as the second noble truth and the cause of suffering. At times, Buddha also referred to the second noble truth as grasping, clinging, and attachment.[2] Sounds a lot like addiction, doesn't it?

When we like something—even when that something isn't good for us, isn't in our best interests, and isn't something we'd let our children do—we nonetheless pursue it. We grasp it and cling to it, ultimately becoming attached to it. In other words, we become addicted. All things considered, we wouldn't be wrong in saying that Buddha identified addiction as the cause of suffering.

Of course, nothing's ever simple. At other times, Buddha identified ignorance as the cause of suffering. And still other times, he spoke of delusion as the cause.[3] Let's look at these two alternatives one at a time.

With ignorance, we lack knowledge. We don't know what we don't know. For example, we don't know the difference between what's good for

---

2   Bhikkhu Bodhi, ed., *In the Buddha's Words: An Anthology of Discourses from the Pali Canon* (Somerville, MA: Wisdom Publications, Inc., 2005), 75–78.

3   "Ignorance: *avijja*," Access to Insight, November 5, 2013, http://www.accesstoinsight.org/ptf/ dhamma/sacca/sacca2/avijja.html.

us and what isn't or between what makes us happy and what doesn't. We don't see the link between our addictive behaviors and our suffering. We don't want to get out of bed in the morning and can't understand why. The fact that we stayed up until 3:00 a.m. playing video games or watching pornography has nothing to do with it, as far as we're concerned. We can't see the connection. That's called ignorance.

With delusion, we think we know what we don't know or that we know more than we actually do know. In other words, we imagine what isn't true to be true. For example, we imagine that having another cookie, another cigarette, or another glass of wine will make us happy. It won't. Believing that it will is called delusion.

We go about our lives guided by these twin deceivers, not knowing how things work but imagining that we do, not knowing how to live, how to succeed, or how to be happy but convincing ourselves or pretending that we do. With ignorance and delusion, we lack insight into the way things work. As a result, we get caught up in the world of addiction. We become attracted and then attached to the wrong things, and so we suffer. To get beyond our suffering and the addictions that feed it, we need to uproot our ignorance and our delusion, replacing them with knowledge and know-how, with insight and wisdom.

To be clear, it isn't having desires that's the culprit. It's having the wrong desires or desiring the wrong things that causes addiction. That's where we get into trouble. To get around this, you'll have to eliminate your old desires while simultaneously cultivating new ones.

Craving, from a Buddhist perspective, is the proximate cause of our suffering, brought on by ignorance and delusion, the root cause of our suffering. We can think of ignorance and delusion as two sides of the same coin. Without this two-sided coin, we'll no longer crave the things to which we've become addicted. In preparing to remove this coin, let's examine two more causal factors: skills and training deficits.

Cultivating a desire is a multistep process, starting with choosing what it is you want to want. Yes, you can choose what you want and what you don't want. If you want to eat burgers and fries, you can replace that desire with the desire to eat fruits and vegetables. Not only can you stop *eating* fatty, salty, sugary foods, you can stop *wanting* to eat them. Not only can you start *eating* more fruits and vegetables, you can start *wanting* to eat them. You can learn to want the things that are in your best long-term interests and to stop wanting those that aren't. You'll start by identifying what those are. What is it you want to want? For example, you might have a friend who gets up early and loves going for a run every morning. You may wish you felt that way about running. You want to get in shape, but you don't want to do what it takes to get there. You wish you wanted to run and go to the gym every day, but you don't.

How you can develop those new and improved desires is coming up shortly. But first, let's continue identifying the causes of your addictions.

A Skills Deficit

From yet another perspective, we suffer because of a skills deficit, which keeps us from thinking and behaving as well as we could. For example, we find ourselves ruminating about the past and worrying about the future. All of us do it to one degree or another, typically because we don't have the tools to stop. It's not hard to see how this kind of thinking leads to suffering. Now we're getting close to the solution: by acquiring the right skills and applying them, we gain knowledge and overcome the ignorance that keeps us trapped in our addictions.

One important skill is the ability to say no. You can think about it this way: Why do we grasp, cling to, and become addicted to things that aren't good for us? Why do we smoke cigarettes, drink beer, or overeat salty, fatty, sugary foods, blissfully ignoring the fact that it's bad for us, somehow convincing ourselves that it's not or that, even if it is, it's still worth doing?

We do it for the same reason we do everything we do: We do it because it feels good. But we also do it because we don't know how not to do it. We don't know how to say no to those guilty pleasures. We lack refusal skills, and that contributes to our addictive behaviors. Even when we decide we no longer want to smoke cigarettes, we don't know how to stop and stay stopped. We keep right on smoking, all the way to the cancer ward. Sound familiar? Addiction becomes a matter of not knowing how to stop. Or maybe more precisely, it's a matter of lacking the skills needed to stop. Lacking those skills is a form of ignorance, a form of ignorance that can and often does turn deadly.

You don't have to be addicted to cigarettes, alcohol, or other drugs—or even things like social media, video games, or cheesecake—to have an addiction. We're addicted to our families, our careers, and our homes. We're addicted to our bodies and the bodies of those we love, or perhaps more accurately, those we've grown attached to. We're addicted to owning nice things and to the nice things we own or think we own. In other words, not only are we addicted to the things we own, but we're also addicted to ownership itself. We're addicted to our histories, our stories, our photo albums, our wedding pictures, our high school yearbook, the way we view ourselves, and the person we fancy ourselves to be. We're addicted to all sorts of things—approval, status, independence, control, power, and life itself. And so, we hold on for dear life, never knowing when it's time to let go, never admitting it when we do know, and refusing to let go when that dreaded day finally arrives, as it inevitably must, as it inevitably will.

As I'll demonstrate, eliminating your vices won't be enough to end your suffering, not nearly enough. Eventually, you have to let go of everything. You can let things go willingly or you can have them taken from you. For example, you can go willingly into old age, or you can be dragged, kicking and screaming. The former requires some skills; the latter does not. Letting go is a skill most of us lack, but it's one that will make your life better in almost every way. Much of what makes our lives a struggle is holding on to things that don't belong to us or can't last beyond their expiration date—for example, remaining young and healthy or having a full head of hair.

As you make your way through this book, you'll learn a specific skill set that will empower you to abandon your vices, bad habits, dependencies, and unhealthy attachments and replace them with healthy alternatives while loving every minute of it. Okay, maybe not every minute but lots of them. Sound good? Keep reading. You'll get there.

A Training Deficit

As you and I have seen, we suffer based on a complex set of causes and conditions. We've looked at suffering from a biological perspective, an evolutionary perspective, an environmental perspective, a psychological perspective, a Buddhist perspective, and from the perspective of a skills deficit. While each of these perspectives plays a role in our suffering, it's the one I'm about to introduce that will provide you with a way out of suffering and addiction, addiction being the brand of suffering we're primarily focused on.

Although suffering and addiction have multiple causes, training is the single solution to overcoming them all. In the pages ahead, you'll learn how to train your way out of your addictions and your suffering. What's needed can be summarized in a simple sentence. Study this important sentence. Memorize it. Contemplate and discuss it—frequently! Ready? Here's the sentence: Training is the key to overcoming addiction and the suffering that comes with it. Read that sentence aloud and remember it.

You have a skills deficit, and that deficit prevents you from making the most of yourself and your life. It leads you away from what's important and what you care deeply about. It leads you from the freedom to do what will make you happy to doing what is sure to make you miserable.

Your skills deficit is the result of a training deficit, which we'll now define as a lack of optimal instruction, practice, coaching, and application of the missing skill set. This is what it takes to overcome an addiction. It's only training that will do the job, and that's what we'll focus on.

Knowing that craving drives your addiction isn't by itself much help, and neither is knowing that you have a skills deficit. The solution is acknowledging you have a training deficit and then engaging wholeheartedly in that training. Only training, the right kind of training, will give you the skills you're missing. Then and only then can you use those skills to eliminate the cravings driving your addictive behaviors and thereby eliminate those addictive behaviors, along with the suffering that comes with them.

While I'll focus on teaching you the skill set, you'll focus on learning and practicing the skill set. Your job is to train and to keep training, using the information presented in this book and the suggested readings. It's only by retraining your thoughts, emotions, and behaviors that you'll free yourself from your addictions. And it's only by freeing yourself from your addictions that you'll free yourself from your suffering.

Freeing yourself from addictions also means replacing them with good habits and the freedom to choose how to live. When you're addicted, you lack that freedom, and without it, suffering is inevitable and happiness impossible.

Going forward, your motto is simple: *More and better training is required!* It's through training that you'll rewire your brain, improve your thinking, eliminate your addictions, and control your behavior.

Yes, your suffering is the result of multiple causes, but you can eliminate each of those causes by focusing primarily on one of them: the training gap and how to close it.

Failure to Follow Through as Cause

Before we move on to the next topic, there's one more thing to consider. It's a habit many of us have developed—the failure to start, continue, or finish the things we claim or once claimed to be committed to. This may be the most important factor of all because if you don't follow through with the instructions detailed in this book, your suffering and addictions will continue to haunt you and keep you trapped in a life barely worth living compared to the life that's possible.

Keep this in mind as you make your way through the book. Follow the instructions, practice the exercises, hire a coach, or learn to coach yourself with help from books or from someone you trust, making sure you *use* what you're learning and apply it to all that you do.

The Goal

With the problem and its causes now in mind, and thus a clear idea of what you *don't* want, it's time to look at what you *do* want. Why do you do the things you do? Specifically, what are you expecting to gain when you indulge in addictive behaviors?

As it turns out, there's only one reason anyone does the things they do. It's why we mainline heroin, smoke cigarettes, drink coffee, or play video games. It's also why we get up in the morning and why we go to bed at night. It's why we show up for work and why we call in sick. It's why we get married and divorced. We do it all for one reason and for one reason only: to change the way we feel—from bad to good or from good to better.

But what exactly do we mean by "good" and "bad" when it comes to feelings, and what do we mean by "feelings"? The Pali and Sanskrit word Buddhists use for feelings is *vedanā*. A more precise definition is feeling tone, which can be either pleasant, unpleasant, or neutral. Human beings, along with all other sentient beings, are naturally drawn toward pleasant feelings. We perk up in their presence. Likewise, we naturally recoil from unpleasant feelings. We avoid them whenever possible. When it comes to neutral feelings, we remain indifferent. We tend to ignore them if we notice them at all.

For our purposes, we'll focus primarily on pleasant and unpleasant feelings and how they relate to addiction. Nothing is as simple as it seems, and this is true for feelings as well.

Good and Bad Feelings

When we say something feels "good," we mean pleasant. When we say it feels "bad," we mean unpleasant. But that doesn't tell you whether what you do to experience those feelings is good or bad for your emotional, mental, or physical health.

Pleasant feelings can be divided into two types: (1) good for you and (2) bad for you. For example, eating a banana not only feels good but is nutritious (good for you). Eating a bowl of ice cream feels good but is sugary (bad for you).

Unpleasant feelings can likewise be divided into the same two types. For example, doing those last two pull-ups gets your muscles working (good for you). Smashing your hand with a hammer harms you (bad for you).

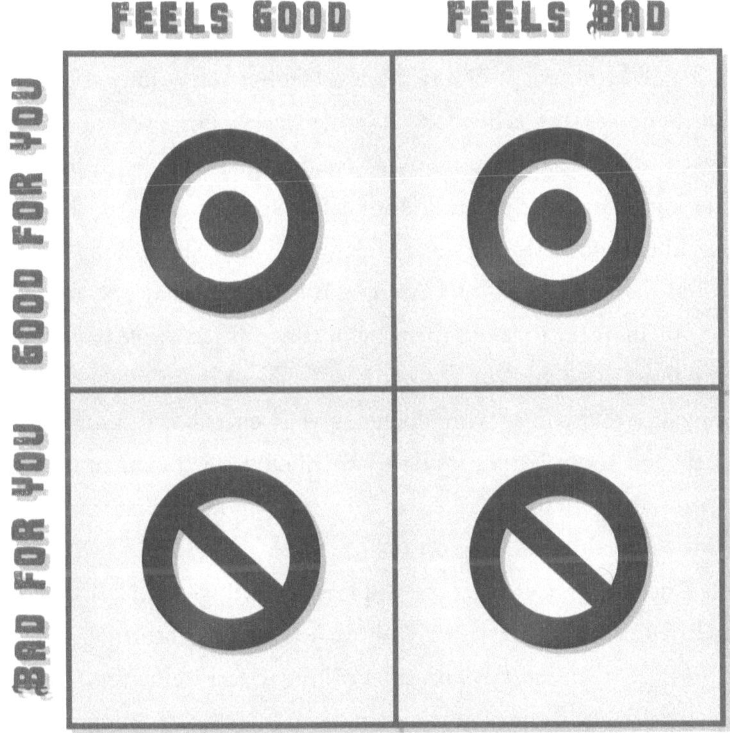

Yes, we all want to feel good and avoid feeling bad. But to get there and to make it genuinely satisfying and lasting, you need to steer clear of the wrong kinds of bad feelings (bad for you) while embracing the right kinds of bad feelings (good for you). Likewise, you need to steer clear of the wrong kind of good feelings (bad for you), while embracing the right kind of good feelings (good for you). Our natural proclivity to favor pleasant over unpleasant feelings is hardwired into our nervous systems. Sometimes it works in our favor. Other times, not so much.

To be successful in life, to get more of what you want and less of what you don't want, you have to master your feelings. That means learning to reject pleasant feelings that are bad for you, while embracing unpleasant feelings that are good for you. At the same time, you need to learn how to avoid bad feelings that are bad for you while embracing bad feelings that are good for you.

But can we realistically embrace a bad feeling? Yes, as long as by "bad" we mean an unpleasant feeling (*vedanā*) that serves a purpose. For example, you'll learn to embrace the unpleasant feelings that come with balancing your checkbook or resisting an offer of cake and ice cream. You'll balance your checkbook and resist the sugary treat, and you'll embrace the unpleasant feelings that come with performing those skillful behaviors. You won't run from them or try to avoid them by putting off the unpleasant task or by giving in to the unhealthy temptation. You'll embrace the boredom or the annoyance that comes with balancing your checkbook, knowing that you'll feel good about it once it's done. You'll embrace the discomfort that comes with saying no to the cake and ice cream, knowing that you'll thank yourself the next time you step on the scale.

You'll no longer try to escape unpleasant feelings. You'll accept and welcome them. You'll investigate and learn from them, turning them to your advantage. That said, you must be willing to feel bad temporarily and embrace unpleasant feelings in the short term in order to overcome them in the long term. Ultimately, unpleasant feelings will no longer bother you. You'll no longer experience them as bad. You'll learn to experience them as good, knowing that the unpleasant feeling may not feel great in the moment but serves a positive purpose.

This won't be easy. The desire to feel good is programmed into our genes. But if we manage to feel good about what's good for us and feel bad about what's bad for us, we'll live another day and be glad we did. I'm not advocating hedonism, nor am I promoting sheer ego gratification. You've already tried all that, and it didn't work. Otherwise, you wouldn't be reading this book.

While pleasure is what you evolved to pursue, you'll have to transcend that evolutionary mandate if you want to be happy. Saying no to a glass of wine or a piece of cheesecake won't feel good, at least not in the short term. Doing your third set of push-ups won't either. Even the first set might not feel good. Do it anyway. Then do the second and the third. Do what's in your best long-term interests, regardless of how it feels or doesn't feel. There's more to living the good life than experiencing pleasure. Let's call it discipline, virtue, and wisdom.

To sum up, we can say there are two types of pleasure: healthy pleasure and unhealthy pleasure. Examples of healthy pleasure include things like the pleasure associated with doing a job well, helping someone in need, or going for a run. Examples of unhealthy pleasure include things like smoking cigarettes, seeking revenge on an enemy, or profiteering.

Feelings Versus Emotions

The distinction between a feeling and an emotion is important. Let's look at it in detail.

By "feeling," we mean a simple sensation that is pleasant, unpleasant, or neutral but no more than that. Emotions (like anger, anxiety, sadness) are more complex. And although unpleasant feelings can be related to suffering, unpleasant feelings do not equate to suffering per se. Suffering, as noted earlier, is always an emotional affair. It's the toxic *emotions* that count as suffering, not the unpleasant feelings that come with toxic emotions. Unpleasant feelings aren't problematic in and of themselves, but toxic emotions are. What we want to avoid, then, is not unpleasant feelings but rather the toxic emotions linked to an unpleasant feeling. Yes, we want to change the way we feel, from bad to good and from good to better, yet not just in the domain of feelings but in the domain of emotions instead.

Unpleasant feelings can come without a related emotion. But toxic emotions always come with unpleasant feelings. Anxiety, for example, is experienced as unpleasant but is much more than that. Unpleasant feelings by themselves aren't necessarily a bad thing and aren't necessarily experienced as suffering. It's the toxic emotions that we experience as suffering. Unpleasant feelings are inevitable. Even Buddha experienced them. But toxic emotions are another story. These we're proposing may not be inevitable. And even if we can't eliminate them altogether, as Buddha is said to have done, we can at least reduce them. That's important for our purposes because toxic emotions often lead to addictive behaviors, behaviors like drinking alcohol that help us repress and escape from the suffering that comes with toxic emotions.

Remember, then, that feelings are simple. There's not much to them, and as I pointed out, they're not always experienced as suffering. And it's suffering, not unpleasant feelings, we want to eliminate. Emotions are much more complicated than mere feelings. Yes, toxic emotions come with an unpleasant feeling, but they come with more than just an unpleasant feeling. They come with an additional set of complex physiological and psychological reactions. For example, our toxic emotions accompany cortisol and other stress hormones that flood our bodies, bringing with them disturbing sensations that are more than just unpleasant feelings. The way we perceive, interpret, judge, and think about those disturbing sensations transforms them from unpleasant feelings into toxic emotions, toxic emotions being another way of saying suffering. It's the combination of stress hormones, distorted perceptions, unskillful interpretations, negative biases, faulty judgments, and yammering cognitions *along with* the unpleasant feelings that add up to suffering. As you can see, unpleasant feelings are just one component among many that make up suffering.

So, it's not simply unpleasant feelings that constitute suffering but rather toxic emotions, toxic emotions being the very definition of suffering, suffering being the one problem we're all trying to solve, the one Buddha labeled the first noble truth, the one trap we're all trying to escape, with addiction being one of the primary causes of our suffering.

In summary, our goal starts with freeing ourselves from toxic emotions, which is another way of saying from suffering. Once we've done that, once we've eliminated the toxic emotions, we'll want to replace them with healthy alternatives. By healthy alternatives, we mean emotions such as gratitude, interest, wonder, enthusiasm, confidence, courage, playfulness, enjoyment, joy, delight, compassion, goodwill, love, harmony, contentment, serenity, equanimity, and other emotions. For the sake of simplicity, we'll refer to healthy emotions in general as happiness, with happiness as a stand-in term for any of the other healthy emotions. Simply put, then, we can say our goal is to be happy, with the understanding that by "happy," we mean emotional well-being of the highest order.

Pleasure Versus Happiness

Pleasure involves good feelings, but happiness is emotional well-being of the highest order—and something to which we all strive. It's happiness we want but not just any old happiness. It's a special kind of happiness, a kind most of us rarely, if ever, experience. In many cases, the happiness most of us experience eventually disappoints because it's not the real thing. It's counterfeit, and counterfeit happiness can't make us, well, happy.

When we use the word "happiness," we mean any healthy, wholesome, life-affirming emotion *along with* the healthy thoughts and behaviors that go with it. We could say our goal is to think, express ourselves, and behave skillfully and with integrity. In that way, we're expressing the goal not as a mere feeling but as a way of being. It's how we feel emotionally and also how we conduct ourselves and respond to the world around us and within us.

Being happy means more than just feeling good. It means doing good! It means doing the right things, at the right time, in the right way, for the right reason. If we *do* that, we'll also *feel* happy. We'll experience positive emotions, including the pleasant feelings that generally come with them. The pleasant feelings we experience while eating cheesecake, scrolling through TikTok, or watching porn don't count as happiness. Your job is to ditch those impostors and replace them with the real thing.

Craving Versus Wanting

Addiction is, to a large extent, a problem of desire. But desire per se isn't the problem. Wrong desire is. Wanting to be a good parent is a healthy desire. Craving a cigarette is an unhealthy desire. You don't *want* a cigarette. You *crave* it. Desire is healthy and wholesome if what you desire is healthy and wholesome. We'll refer to this type of desire as wanting. Desire is unhealthy and unwholesome if what you desire is unhealthy and unwholesome. (If what you desire is unattainable, this also counts as unhealthy.) We'll refer to this type of desire as craving.

You *want* a good education, meaningful work, and a safe place to live. If you have children, you want your children to be safe and happy. These are the types of things you *want*. On the other hand, you *crave* a cigarette, a glass of wine, a pot of coffee, or another cookie. These are the types of things we crave, deluding ourselves into believing we want them. Most smokers wish they could stop, but they don't know how. They reluctantly continue, hoping that one day they'll be able to quit.

It's important to learn to distinguish between what you want and what you crave. You *crave* things like cigarettes, a pot of coffee, and a box of crackers. You *want* things like a college degree, a meaningful career, and a safe place to live. Desire comes in these two main types, what we want and what we crave. You'll want to zero in on the former and move away from the latter and be sure to avoid craving even the wholesome things you want. Craving itself is problematic, regardless of what you're craving.

When you *want* something, you see it as an objective worthy of pursuing. When it's something you *crave*, the thing you crave pursues you. If you crave cigarettes, for example, that's the tobacco industry coming after you with their goal of hooking you on their product. If they win, you'll be paying them to reach their goal of making a profit while you kill yourself using their product. Cravings are innately destructive. That's the difference.

Knowing what you want starts with knowing what you don't want. In other words, discovering what your goal is starts with discovering what it isn't, and it isn't getting the things you crave. Contrary to popular belief, your goal isn't to avoid disadvantage or gain advantage. It's not to avoid hassles, disappointments, or setbacks. It's not even to avoid tragedy, crisis, or catastrophe. In other words, it's not to avoid adversity. Nor is it to get to work on time or make your boss happy or win employee of the year. The goal isn't to win friends and influence people, get married, own a house, or raise a family. It's not to win the lottery. Your goals are not any of the things you may imagine them to be.

What you and I and everyone else truly wants is to feel the way we imagine having those things will make us feel. That is what we want. Underneath it all, we just want to feel good. Learning to do that in a reliable, responsible, and sustainable way is what this book is about. And learning to do it starts with understanding that the things we think will make us happy won't. We want to be happy—but happy in the best sense of the word.

Remember we do the things we do to change the way we feel from bad to good or from good to better. Again, that's it. That's all we ever want, not a new car, not a bigger house in an upscale neighborhood, not the perfect wife or the perfect husband, not even healthy, happy, well-behaved children. We want the good feelings we imagine having those things will bring us. But even those good feelings aren't what we really want because those types of good feeling are unpredictable, unreliable, and unsustainable.

What we really want are good feelings that are predictable, reliable, and sustainable. Once you understand that, you have a shot at getting what you *really* want. Without that understanding, the ultimate goal of happiness and freedom will continue to elude you. Identifying the right kind of good feelings (*healthy emotions with or without pleasant feeling tones*) and learning to elicit them on command without resorting to unskillful means are the secrets to becoming and remaining vice-free.

Our goal is to put an end to the suffering that comes with being addicted (and attached). We'll do this by becoming and remaining vice-free and thereby free of the suffering that comes with being controlled by our vices.

The Plan

We've identified the problem. We know the cause. We have our goal. Now, we need a plan. And our plan can be summed up with two words: abandon and develop.

If the reason we do anything is the reason we do everything (and it is), and if we know what that reason is (and we do), we can use it to guide our behavior. We can use the way we feel as our North Star, directing us to move away from toxic environments and reactions toward healthy alternatives.

To do this successfully, we'll have to override natural selection, which cares only that we survive and reproduce. By choosing which kinds of feelings to avoid and which kinds of feelings to embrace, we can transcend our natural predilections for good feelings that aren't always good for us. Remember the four kinds of feelings: feels good/good for you, feels good/bad for you, feels bad/bad for you, and feels bad/good for you.

As we now know, not all feelings are created equal, so we need a way to change the way we feel from bad to good or from good to better without relying on any vices to do it. In other words, we want to change the way we feel without dipping into those good feelings that are bad for us and without avoiding those bad feelings that are good for us. We'll start by renouncing our vices (abandon) and replacing them with virtues (develop).

Applying this simple strategy to our lives gives us the best chance of overcoming our vices and realizing our highest aspirations. The rest of this book will provide you with a plan to do just that.

3

PLEASE DON'T CALL
IT A DISEASE

People don't drink because they're alcoholics.
They're alcoholics because they drink.

—Tat Twam, One of the Deadly Dogs

One night not long after I graduated from high school, my best friend Steve Brookings and I sat in his beat-up Ford Custom smoking a joint when we noticed a sign for a new business. This was the section of my hometown of Burlington, Massachusetts, where my druggie friends, as my mother liked to call them, and I hung out. We knew this strip like the backs of our hands, so even stoned, or perhaps especially stoned, we were sure to notice anything new or different.

The sign had a tiger painted on one side, a dragon on the other, and in between, the words "Kenpo Karate Jujitsu Kung Fu." It seemed my hometown was about to get its first martial arts studio! This was the early 1970s, and thanks to the popularity of the television series *Kung Fu* and the emergence of Bruce Lee and his groundbreaking movie *Enter the Dragon,* martial arts were making the scene in the United States.

If you're not familiar with the show, *Kung Fu* was a hit TV series that followed the adventures of Kwai Chang Caine, a humble half-American, half-Chinese Shaolin monk who wanders from town to town in the Old West kicking the crap out of bullies and racists—but only after they attacked him or some defenseless bystander. Steve and I both watched the show every week at my mother's house and fell in love with kung fu.

Stoned and reading the new sign through the windshield of Steve's car, I said, " I have no idea what kenpo is. But karate is when you use a karate chop to break boards or knock your opponents out with a karate chop to the back of the neck."

"Jujitsu," I went on, "is when you touch someone on a pressure point, and he collapses. And kung fu is when you rip out someone's heart!" Thanks to the show *Kung Fu*, both Steve and I were as curious about the martial arts as we were clueless.

The next day, Steve and I returned to Burlington center to check out this mysterious new martial arts studio. We were greeted by a very intimidating guy, who was older and much bigger than both of us, and Steve was no half-pint. I weighed about 130 pounds at 5'8" at the time, and this man looked at least twice my size. Later we learned his name was Rudy Horn, and he was a third-degree black belt.

"Can I help you, gentlemen?" Rudy asked, obviously not impressed with our long hair and black leather jackets.

"Yeah," I said, "We want to hear your spiel." I don't know why I said that. I certainly wasn't trying to be cocky. It was obviously out of nervousness.

A hard look washed over Rudy's face. "How about I *show* you my spiel?" he replied.

Steve was standing behind me with his extended arm propped against the doorframe, blocking the entrance. I turned, ducked under his arm, and headed out the door as fast as I could. Steve quickly followed. When we got back to the car, we tried to figure out what went wrong and concluded I sounded as if I was being cocky. Rudy must have thought we were messing with him.

But we were genuinely interested in learning martial arts, and the next day Steve went back to the studio. He explained to Rudy that I had felt nervous, not cocky, and that's why we got off on the wrong foot. He convinced Rudy that we both wanted to take lessons. Then he came and persuaded me that it was safe to go back to the studio to sign up.

We started taking lessons, and I soon learned something about myself: I had never learned how to learn. The truth is, I'd made it through the public school system without learning much of anything. Part of this fell squarely on the shoulders of my teachers and parents. At teacher-parent conferences all through grammar school, my mother would ask, "What are we going to do with him?" Well, neither my mother nor my teachers ever figured out what to do with me, other than make me stand in the corner and stay after school. My mother was too overwhelmed dealing with six children and an inebriated husband to make me do my homework, much less help me with it. I spent most of my time at school staring out the window. After school, I read comic books, watched TV, and listened to my parents fight.

By the time I got to junior high and then high school, I was placed in the classes for "slow" students and pushed through the system. In high school, I joined the Work Study Program, which meant I left school early to go to work as a stock boy. The few classes I attended were a joke. My English teacher read the paper during class. I'd bring him coffee, which meant I'd get a good grade. On test days, he'd go around to each desk and put the test question on our desks. When he got to me, he'd turn the paper over to the blank side and say, "Draw me some tattoos."

I drew him tattoos and got a B in English.

After I graduated from high school, I lived with my parents, and my mother kept telling me to get a job. "What are you going to do with yourself?" she yelled. In other words, my mother was still asking, "What are we going to do with him?"

Honestly, it was a good question. I wasn't feeling too good about my life either. I still mainly hung out with my druggie friends, getting high, listening to music, and chasing girls. I'd had a few gigs as a janitor, pushing a broom and emptying wastebaskets, but my only interests were sex, drugs, and rock 'n' roll. I had no other interests. I never played or even watched a sport in my life. I had no idea what a career was or how to go about getting one.

At that point, even I was asking myself, "What are we going to do with him?"

And then came the martial arts studio, and it was there, for the first time, that I finally started learning something. First, basic punches and kicks, then drilling them over and over. It was something I had never done before: practice! Every week, Steve and I would take our lesson and practice what we learned. As we advanced, we learned combinations of strikes and kicks, put together as real self-defense techniques. Next, we learned our first kata. A kata is a dance-like exercise that brings together all the elements we had learned so far. This was a complex set of movements that I found challenging both to learn and perform. This learning business was all new to me.

But I persisted.

I began to understand that learning is a systematic, step-by-step process that involves rehearsing the same thing repeatedly until it sinks in. Then it hit me that it was like learning math, which I never bothered to do. But the idea was the same. You learn addition and subtraction, then move on to multiplication and division, then fractions and algebra, and it keeps getting more and more advanced until you face something incomprehensible, like calculus. These were all the subjects I avoided because they seemed irrelevant, not to mention difficult if not impossible for me to learn. But now here I was in a dojo learning martial arts and, for the first time in my life, learning about learning.

I absolutely loved it! You could say I became addicted to learning.

It was at the martial arts studio that I also learned about discipline. For me, discipline was what happened when I got in trouble at school. I got hit with a ruler or told to stand in the corner. But now I was learning about self-discipline, and it was how I would direct myself to do the work of learning, practicing, and mastering a skill set—in this case, kenpo, karate, jujitsu, and kung fu. I was on my way to a whole new life, a whole new me, which included opening and operating a martial arts studio of my own and eventually giving up the drugs and alcohol (more on how I did that in the coming chapters).

Later, in my early 30s, I retired from my martial arts career and went on to college, where I brought my love of learning and discipline with me. When I graduated with the highest honors, I thought, "Oh wow, if my public schoolteachers could see me now." I went on to get a master's degree in counseling psychology and soon got a job as a mental health and addictions counselor. It was there that I cemented the connection between addiction and learning. Addiction, it became clear, is the result of learning.

Getting sober follows the same path. We have to learn how to get and stay sober, just as we learned how to become addicted—through work and practice. Toward that end, in this chapter, we'll expose the myths surrounding alcoholism and other addictions. Yes, myths. Most, if not all, of what we've been told about addiction is wrong. Let's see if we can straighten that out by giving you a clearer understanding of why you attach yourself to unhealthy behaviors and become addicted, so you can learn to detach.

The Disease Model

Let's identify what it is we're dealing with when we use terms like "alcoholism" and "alcoholic," or more broadly, "addiction" and "addict." We'll start by considering the ever-popular disease model of addiction. And I'll argue that addiction is not what we've been led to believe it is.

That alcoholism is a medical condition, a chronic relapsing brain disease, remains an entrenched dogma that rarely gets challenged by mental health professionals or their clients. They live in a culture and work in a system that embraces the disease model. It may be all they know. But although it's clearly the most popular theory related to addiction, not to mention depression, anxiety, and a whole host of other human emotions and behaviors, it's certainly not the best. In fact, it's arguably the worst.

Why?

Referring to these psychological phenomena as medical conditions distracts and misdirects our attention from the real causes and solutions. Government funding goes to researching diseases that don't exist, instead of spending that money on researching the underlying reasons for toxic emotions and addictive behaviors. By treating these emotional and behavioral experiences as medical conditions, we make these problems worse, not better, and guarantee more, not less, suffering for more and more people.[4]

If we, as a society, and if you, as an individual, have any chance of overcoming the problem of addiction, we had better know what we're dealing with. Are we dealing with a medical condition that calls for a medical solution? Or are we dealing with a psychological problem that calls for a psychological solution? Getting the right answer is critical not only for individuals suffering from addiction but for their family members, employers, and communities as well.

Let's dive right in and see what a little common sense tells us.

Drinking yourself into a drunken stupor isn't a disease. It's a choice, a choice followed by intentional behavior. We don't need to implicate genetics, brain chemistry, metabolites, or any of the other usual suspects. Drinking alcohol is a voluntary, self-selected, and self-initiated behavior. That's all you need to know. Things like genetics, brain chemistry, and metabolism all play a role in this and all our other behaviors, but we have no need to consider their role here. In the same way that you can drive a car without any knowledge of combustion engines, transmissions, or anything else under the hood, so too can you control your behavior without knowing anything about genetics, brain chemistry, or metabolism. These topics may be interesting and may even provide fascinating insights into your behavior. But when it comes to understanding what causes addiction, those types of insights are the booby prize.

Knowing what role genetics, brain chemistry, or biology plays in your drinking problem will *not* help you stop drinking, although knowing what you *think* about and how you *feel* about those factors might. Still, it's your

---

4   See *Anatomy of an Epidemic: Magic Bullets, Psychiatric Drugs, and the Astonishing Rise of Mental Illness in America* by Robert Whitaker.

subjective experience of what's happening—not which chemicals are flowing through your brain while you're having those experiences—that *you* should be concerned about.

While there's a huge hubbub surrounding neuroscience these days, it's cognitive science that we'll primarily draw on. In other words, it's the mind—not the brain—we should focus on when it comes to understanding and solving the problems of addiction and the suffering (hangovers, regret, guilt, shame, anxiety, depression, etc.) that comes with it.

If you drink too much, you've likely been told that you're suffering from a disease called alcoholism. It's likely you've also been told that because it's a disease, using willpower to address it will only end in frustration and failure. After all, the argument goes, you wouldn't try to use willpower to cure diarrhea, would you? This is an argument that proponents of the disease model often like to make. But there's one big problem with their argument: It's wrong. It's wrong because it's based on the false premise that drinking alcohol is like having diarrhea. The comparison isn't even close. Unlike drinking alcohol, diarrhea *is* a medical condition. And unlike drinking alcohol, it's also an involuntary condition.

I'll say it again. Drinking alcohol is *not* a medical condition. It's a behavior—a voluntary, self-selected, deliberate, intentional behavior, and an unskillful behavior performed with the best of intentions. While we *don't* choose to have diarrhea, we *do* choose to have a drink and then another and another until we become intoxicated. That's not a disease with which we've been inflicted. It's a vice we indulge in.

If you want to overcome your addictions, you'll need to be clear about a few things. First, understand that activities such as smoking cigarettes, drinking alcohol, taking drugs, surfing the internet, gaming, gambling, viewing pornography, and shoplifting are not medical conditions. If you smoke cigarettes, drink alcohol, spend your hard-earned money on scratch tickets, inject heroin, watch X-rated videos, or swipe clothing from your local department store, you are not the victim of a medical condition. You are the perpetrator of unskillful, irresponsible, self-limiting, self-sabotaging, self-defeating, and, in some cases, unethical, immoral, antisocial, or illegal behavior.

It's also called bad behavior. That's right. When you do these things, you're engaging in bad behavior. But, and this is important, this is not to say that *you* are a bad *person*. It is to say you're *behaving* badly and that you're responsible and accountable for that behavior and its consequences. We'll discuss more about this distinction between you and your behavior and its importance in a bit.

The idea of alcoholism as a disease was popularized by Alcoholics Anonymous. Within the traditional 12-step recovery movement, alcohol is described as powerful, cunning, baffling, and insidious while you, a poor victim of the so-called incurable disease that comes with alcohol, are said to be powerless. But just as drinking too much alcohol isn't a disease, neither is alcohol the intelligent entity described above. How could alcohol be cunning or insidious? A bottle of wine possesses no such qualities. Cunning is a function of intelligence. No intelligence, no cunning.

What *is* powerful, cunning, baffling, and insidious is the mind of someone who thinks and drinks themselves into a drunken stupor. Imagine being so cunning that you can talk yourself into engaging in this kind of self-destructive behavior—as if it were a good idea! Now *that's* powerful. *That's* cunning, baffling, and insidious.

Another major tenet of the traditional recovery movement is the idea of powerlessness. As a victim of the "disease of alcoholism," you are said to be powerless. This means you are incapable of deciding to stop drinking. According to this model, you are under the control of an irresistible force. You have lost all choice in the matter of drinking alcohol. You have an overwhelming compulsion to drink, and no amount of commitment, determination, or willpower can stop you. Clearly, the tail is wagging the dog.

Fortunately, as we'll discuss in more detail, this is simply not the case. On the contrary, you are the instigator and the perpetrator of your drinking or whatever vice in which you happen to indulge. You—or more accurately, a part of you—possess the power that initiates and carries out the behavior. If you so choose, you can stop engaging in this self-initiated, self-sabotaging, and self-defeating activity, provided you make the choice and then follow it with action. That action, however, must include acquiring the right mindset and the right skill set, which is precisely what this book is designed to help you do.

None of this is to say it will be easy or that there aren't other contributing factors. It won't be, and there are. Unlearning well-established habits is rarely, if ever, easy. When those habits provide relief from discomfort, that makes it even more difficult. Add to that the pleasure that typically follows that relief, and you're dealing with a formidable opponent indeed. Not a medical opponent, mind you, but a deeply entrenched habit that you've become addicted to performing. Addiction is a habit among habits, a super habit so entrenched that it seems to have a will of its own, the important word here being "seems."

Along with what seems to me to be common sense, treatment outcome studies indicate that medication is not effective in treating not only alcoholism but also depression, anxiety, and other proposed diseases. In his excellent book *Anatomy of an Epidemic: Magic Bullets, Psychiatric Drugs, and the Astonishing Rise of Mental Illness in America,* journalist and author Robert Whitaker reports on a 15-year federally funded study. In the study, patients with schizophrenia and manic depression who stayed off psychiatric medications fared better than those who remained on them.[5] He also quotes an editorial in the *Journal of Child and Adolescent Psychopharmacology,* which read "There is no escaping the fact that research studies certainly have not supported the efficacy of tricyclic antidepressants in treated depressed adolescents."[6]

I must admit that I have seen medication work wonders for clients of mine with bipolar disorder, so it's important to keep an open mind and explore all possible avenues to recovery.

With that said, why is medication so often ineffective in treating these

---

5   Robert Whitaker, *Anatomy of an Epidemic: Magic Bullets, Psychiatric Drugs, and the Astonishing Rise of Mental Illness in America* (New York: Crown Publishers, 2010), loc. 83–86 of 303, Kindle.

6   Whitaker, *Anatomy of an Epidemic,* loc. 169 of 303, Kindle.

conditions? Medication is ineffective when we deal with emotional and behavioral conditions, conditions that arise in the wake of difficult life circumstances. When this is the case, psychological, not medical, interventions are appropriate.

Suffering, by the way, is also not a medical condition. It's an emotional condition, one that responds to psychological interventions, such as the ones you'll learn about in the pages of this book. (Also, if you have emotional problems along with addiction, there's good news ahead.)

Treating addictive behaviors with medication as if they *were* medical conditions is, in my view, a colossal blunder and, in some cases, a calculated misdeed. Prescribing medication for nonmedical conditions is unethical. Overprescribing them for the purpose of lining one's pockets is downright criminal, especially when children are involved.

According to Whitaker, pharmaceutical companies first started prescribing stimulants to children diagnosed with hyperactivity in the 1980s.[7] Next, psychiatrists began prescribing selective serotonin reuptake inhibitors (SSRIs) to teenagers in the 1990s.[8] And in 1997, Whitaker writes, "The *Wall Street Journal* reported that manufacturers of SSRIs were 'taking aim at a controversial new market: children.'"[9]

Whitaker goes on to say that, according to an article in the *New York Times*, this new initiative was driven by drug companies looking to expand their market.[10] Whitaker also cites studies that show participants taking psychotropic medications for depression, bipolar disorder, and even schizophrenia typically fared worse than those not using the drugs.[11] This evidence suggests that these disorders are psychological, not biological, in nature. If you're still not convinced, I suggest you read Whitaker's book.

Now don't get me wrong. I'm not saying that *all* prescribers of psychiatric medications are miscreants only out to make a profit, though some

---

7   Whitaker, *Anatomy of an Epidemic.*
8   Whitaker, *Anatomy of an Epidemic,* loc. 176 of 303, Kindle.
9   Whitaker, *Anatomy of an Epidemic,* loc. 235 of 303, Kindle.
10   Whitaker, *Anatomy of an Epidemic,* loc. 235 of 303, Kindle.
11   Whitaker, *Anatomy of an Epidemic,* loc. 83–86 of 303, Kindle.

surely are. It's safe to say that some psychiatrists and psychopharmacologists are hardworking, caring professionals who, while striving to be of service and often providing that service, are also unknowingly caught up in a corrupt system. Psychopharmacology is big business, plain and simple. Profit driven, it has made a strong case for its products, and most people, including most mental health professionals, sincerely but mistakenly believe that psychiatric medications are a legitimate treatment for the human condition. They most often are not. The human condition is not improved by dulling the mind with mind-altering substances. It's improved by training, not drugging, the mind.

I'm also not saying that the founders of Alcoholics Anonymous (AA) had malevolent intentions when they defined alcoholism as a disease. It's an idea that sometimes helps people make sense of their drinking, or more accurately, what seems like sense. Disease, as a metaphor, can even have value. Unlike those who prescribe psychotropic medications, those who prescribe attendance at AA meetings and the 12-step practice do a world of good for those who follow that advice. Following the 12 steps is an example of training the mind.

The problem is, like every other system, including the system detailed in this book, AA is not a perfect one. Not everyone benefits from its approach, just as not everyone will benefit from the approach detailed here. Some people in AA just can't buy the disease concept or the idea that they are powerless over their own behavior. Others don't believe the notion that there is a God who will cure their disease and remove their shortcomings if they just have faith.

As for the system detailed in this book, not everyone will agree that addiction, depression, anxiety, and other emotional and behavioral problems aren't medical conditions requiring medication. Each of us must come to our own conclusions and choose our own path to recovery. If you do decide to go the medication route, however, I suggest you be an informed consumer. Start by reading Robert Whitaker's excellent book and learn all you can about any drug you plan to take before taking it.

And don't stop there. Educate yourself about both sides of the argument. You may decide I'm wrong about the disease model. Don't take my word for it. Be an informed consumer, then put to the test whichever approach you decide to follow.

Remember, we're most interested in finding what *works*.

If you are someone who doesn't believe in the disease model, in taking psychotropic medications, in powerlessness, or in a God who will answer your prayers, there are other approaches that can and will work for you. And even if you *are* a believer in those ideas, you can still benefit from the alternative ideas detailed in this and other books. (See appendix A.) But again, it's not about what we believe. It's about what works. You don't have to believe that eating less and exercising more will help you lose weight. You just have to do it. Believe it or not, eating less and exercising more takes off the pounds. And in a similar fashion, following the instructions detailed in this book can free you from the stranglehold of your addictions—no medication needed.

You may be asking, "Don't mental health experts believe that alcoholics suffer from a bona fide medical condition?" No, they don't. While the American Society of Addiction Medicine recognizes addiction as a disease, not everyone agrees. For example, the National Institute on Drug Abuse defines "addiction" as a "chronic, relapsing disorder."[12] Notice that, along with using the term "disorder," they also use the term "drug abuse" in their title when describing the problem of drug addiction. Calling addiction a disorder and using the terms "use" and "abuse" is an improvement. But I contend we can go one better by calling it essentially a learned behavior and a choice among options, though not without other contributing factors adding to the mix.

This definition feels more optimistic about one's chances of recovering—that is, of unlearning our addictive behaviors and replacing them with nonaddictive, self-empowering alternatives. It puts the ball in the court of

---

12   "What Is Drug Addiction?," National Institute on Drug Abuse, July 2020, https://nida.nih.gov/publications/drugs-brains-behavior-science-addiction/drug-misuse-addiction.

the person with the addiction. It makes each of us responsible for our addictive behaviors and empowers us to do whatever it takes to eliminate them. If our addictive behaviors are something we've learned and choices we make, then we can unlearn those behaviors, learn new behaviors, and make healthy choices going forward. This doesn't mean we have to do it alone or that we can't ask for help. We can, and in most cases, we should.

I previously worked as a licensed alcohol and drug addiction counselor as well as the director of addictions services for a large social service agency, and I'm one of the many addiction specialists who never bought into the dubious idea that being addicted to drinking alcohol or taking any other drug is a disease. These are behaviors, and behaviors are not medical conditions. If you want to overcome your drinking problem or any addiction, there are a few things you'd better be clear about.

Regardless of what experts say or don't say, common sense and a little reflection confirms that activities such as smoking cigarettes, drinking alcohol, taking drugs, viewing pornography, and shoplifting are not medical conditions. If you smoke cigarettes, drink alcohol, snort cocaine, inject heroin, watch porn, spend your hard-earned money on scratch tickets, or swipe clothing from your local department store, you are *not* the victim of a medical condition. You are the perpetrator of bad behavior that has consequences you'd be better off without.

As I said before—and this is important—doing these things does not make you a bad person. After all, how could a bad person ever perform a good deed? And we all perform some good and some not-so-good deeds. Indulging in addictive behaviors goes in the bad-deed column. But labeling yourself a bad person would be an overgeneralization, and believing it would make it impossible for you to perform good deeds, like giving up your addictions. Let's not confuse the deed with the person. It remains true, however, that you are engaging in bad behavior, that you are responsible and accountable for that behavior and its consequences, and that you have a responsibility to stop.

That you're not the victim of a medical condition isn't to say you're not *addicted* to your chosen vice or that you can simply decide to give it up. You're up against a complicated condition that includes your own biology, learning history, entrenched beliefs, and a culture of quick fix thinkers that includes most people. Those quick fix thinkers are especially prone to buying into the idea that there's a magic pill for every problem. In renouncing your addictions, you'll surely meet with great resistance, not only from yourself but also from those around you as well.

You live in a culture where most of your friends, family, and coworkers are likely to be deeply entrenched in addictions of their own. If they're not addicted to illicit drugs, they're likely to be hooked on sugar, caffeine, nicotine, alcohol, "medical" marijuana, Ritalin, Adderall, Prozac, oxycodone, fentanyl, or one or more of the other growing numbers of legal drugs.

If they're not addicted to one or more of these legal or illegal drugs, they're likely to be addicted to watching TV, buying scratch tickets, hanging out on social media, or any of the other countless activities that people habitually turn to for relief from suffering. These behaviors are so common and so widely accepted that your resolve to get off the merry-go-round will be met with bewilderment by some and hostility by others. How to deal with these saboteurs will be explained in an upcoming chapter.

But now, let's look at the alternative model we'll be using in this book.

The Breakaway Recovery Model

Okay, I hope I've made my point: Addiction is not a medical condition or a chronic, relapsing brain disease. Let's do away with that definition once and for all, defining it instead as a learned behavior and a choice among options. Until new evidence indicates otherwise, that will be our working definition. Defining addiction in this way will lead us to a workable solution.

Addictive behaviors are activities you do voluntarily. Against your better judgment? Most likely. Automatically? You bet. Absentmindedly? Sure thing. Regretfully? Let's hope so. But in each case, you do it because you choose to do it, and you choose to do it because it feels good or because it used to feel good, and you're hoping against hope that it will get you back to feeling good. It won't—at least, not for long. Not if it's an addiction you're dealing with, it won't, and not before delivering a boatload of nasty consequences.

Addiction is also a learned behavior, and learning takes place when a behavior is performed and when that behavior gets rewarded or punished. When repeated, a behavior lays down neural pathways in the central nervous system, making the behavior easier to remember and easier to perform in the future. Behaviors that get rewarded get repeated because we learn how to perform the behavior and learn it has a desirable payoff. Behaviors that get punished are less likely to be repeated. If it feels good, we're likely to do it again. If it feels bad, not so much. In other words, you don't drink because you're an alcoholic. You're an alcoholic because you drink, and you drink because drinking makes you feel good, at least for a while.

Over time, we become addicted to behaviors that make us feel good. When performing a behavior feels really good—smoking crack, for example—that's when addiction is most likely to set in. Not because smoking crack is a disease, mind you, but rather because smoking crack *feels so damn good*. If you want to overcome your addictions, it will help to know that you're addicted because you repeatedly engage in a pleasure-producing behavior. Your addiction is the result of the highly rewarding nature of this behavior.

Even if you can't agree with that definition of addiction as a chosen, learned behavior and not a chronic medical condition, you'll find helpful information in this book. If you follow its instructions, your chances of overcoming your addictions will increase dramatically, whether you subscribe to this theory of addiction or not. It will help. What is necessary is doing the work. What work? Study, practice, practice, practice, and application of the strategies, tactics, tools, and techniques of *Breakaway Recovery*.

Now, let's look at why letting go of our addictive behaviors is so challenging and what makes us feel as if we're powerless victims of a brain disease that requires medical interventions.

In chapter 1, where we looked at the causes and conditions of suffering, we noted that there are multiple causes and conditions and that those same causes and conditions that cause suffering also cause addiction. While addiction isn't a medical condition, it does have its roots in biology and in our evolutionary past. Natural selection built us to crave what feels good and to avoid what doesn't. On top of that, our natural inclination to develop addictions is exacerbated by our learning histories, our environments, and by a skills deficit so immense we could lead a herd of elephants through it.

We all have these glaring deficits to one degree or another and more than we realize. We never learned how to resist temptation, and we routinely experience temptations that are extremely difficult and often seemingly impossible to resist. In this modern world, some of these temptations involve abnormally intense—or supernormal—stimuli that our ancestors never encountered in the environment they inhabited, the environment our brains evolved in.

Pornography is one of those many supernormal stimuli. Nowhere in the natural world will you find access to hundreds of people eager to gratify you sexually with every sex act you can imagine, and some you never would have imagined, had you not stumbled upon them on the internet. Our brains come hardwired to seek variety and novelty when it comes to finding mates. But the brain never evolved to handle the kind of variety and novelty found in pornography. Watching pornography overwhelms the brain, causing it to overdose on dopamine—the search, find, and remember neurotransmitter—along with a host of other pleasure-producing neurotransmitters that reward us. Of course, you're not having real sex with real people. You're having sex alone while looking at a screen. But your brain doesn't know that, so it responds as it would to the real thing.

Here's the problem: If we continue to indulge in these unnaturally pleasant behaviors, we're bound to overdose on dopamine and the cocktail of chemicals responsible for rewarding us. We also deplete our brain's supply of these important neurochemicals. Over time, we require more variety, more novelty, and more intensity.

If you're a porn addict and you're married, you've long ago lost interest in having sex with your spouse in favor of masturbating to images on a screen. But soon, even those images will no longer be enough. Tolerance has made you immune to the natural sights and sounds that once sexually aroused you. Your addiction to sex via pornography has also reached a point of diminishing returns, leaving you incapable of becoming sexually aroused or being aroused only by increasingly novel and intense pornographic images.

A new generation of adolescents growing up watching porn from an early age often have little interest in having sex with real people. They've been conditioned over hundreds of hours of watching porn to seek and enjoy images on a screen, not in the flesh. They don't know how to relate to a real person sexually, so they resign themselves to a life of porn addiction with little or no hope of ever finding a mate. And because their porn use has become a bona fide addiction, they will experience the inevitable suffering that comes with addictive behavior.

They depend on porn for relief from cravings and for pleasure. Over time, as with all addictions, they need more and more to get the relief and pleasure they crave. The more they indulge, the less satisfying it becomes, and the more they need to indulge to get the same amount of relief and pleasure. Sooner or later, no amount does the trick. They can no longer get the relief and pleasure they crave. At best, it's diminished in duration and intensity, so it never quite satisfies the way it once did. Ironically, their enjoyment diminishes while their craving increases. It satisfies them less while their desire to be satisfied grows stronger. Yes, it's a nightmare.

But that's not the end of it. If you're addicted to porn, you not only lose interest in having sex with real people, but you also lose interest in everything else in your life. As your porn addiction depletes your happy brain chemicals, you'll lose your drive to pursue your other interests. Porn becomes the focus of your life. You'll find that your other interests can't compete with such unnaturally intense stimuli.

This happens suddenly in some cases, gradually in others. You might not see it coming. But it's coming. You begin to notice that you're not as motivated as you once were to get that college degree, start that business, or even go to the gym. You lack motivation for the things that matter most, and when you do manage to engage in these activities, they're not as satisfying as they once were.

There's no getting around it: If you want to feel good, anything you engage in obsessively must go, whether it's porn or Twitter, if you want to enjoy your life and realize your potential. Social media sites are purposely designed to suck you in and keep you coming back. It's not that you can't use these sites deliberately and responsibly, but most users don't. Most users are manipulated by positive and negative reinforcements built into the sites.

The first step is realizing that what you're doing destroys any chance you have of being happy and building a life worth living. If you watch porn or engage in any other addictive behavior, you're damaging your brain. You're overtaxing your brain's motivation and reward centers. You're depleting your brain's happy chemicals, leaving you feeling less motivated to do the things you really care about and less satisfied than you could be when you do manage to do them. You become a shadow of the person you could be.

When you consistently engage with an unnaturally intense stimulus, your other interests can't help but pale in comparison. Going to the gym no longer interests you. Your spouse no longer attracts you. That novel you wanted to write loses its appeal. Why sit and do all that hard work when you can simply turn on your computer and, with a few clicks of the mouse, flood your mind with images of the most beautiful people on the planet?

Activities like taking drugs, playing video games, and watching pornography occupy your time and attention even when you're not indulging in them. Whatever your vice, you spend a significant amount of time thinking about it, resisting it, chasing it, obtaining it, indulging in it, and recovering from it. It uses up your time and attention along with your happy brain chemicals. Just as there are only so many hours in a day, there's only so much time for happiness in a lifetime.

Your brain, over the years, can produce limited blasts of happy chemicals. There is a cap on how much dopamine, serotonin, oxytocin, endorphin, and other happy chemicals you have at your disposal. You want to be thoughtful about how and when your brain dispenses them.

You'll want to get the most bang for your buck. If you spend your precious time online, your brain's reward system is being run down. You're exhausting it, and you're taking time and energy away from the people and activities that really matter and would bring you real happiness, not the counterfeit kind you get from mind-numbing addictive behaviors.

If you want to get the most out of your brain and your life, you have to take better care of both. That includes exercising, getting enough sleep, meditating, and eating unprocessed, plant-based whole foods, and pursuing the projects that light you up. And of course, you'll have to abandon your addictive behaviors, those behaviors that tax your brain's motivation and reward circuits, leaving you too worn out to pursue what really matters. Taking care of your brain includes training yourself to enjoy simple, wholesome pleasures and to pursue the people and pastimes that light you up and help you achieve lasting success and happiness.

Did you get that? Something better lies in store for you than sitting in front of a screen and numbing yourself out when you could be creating the life of your dreams. Living the dream is not just for a chosen few. It's not something that chooses you. It's something you choose to do. You can choose to spend your time playing video games or sitting in front of a TV. Or you can choose to spend your time creating your masterpiece, whatever that is for you. For some, it's going back to school to finish that degree. For others, it's embarking on their ideal career. For still others, it's writing the next great American novel. There's a whole world of unexplored, undiscovered possibilities out there, just waiting for you to wake up and discover it.

Addiction is an attempted solution to the problem of suffering and all of its related feelings, from anxiety to depression. We turn to our vices to escape those unpleasant feelings, and we make matters worse, not better. But we can do better. You can do better. Keep reading!

Standard Addiction Criteria

During intake, most addiction counselors and addiction treatment facilities use certain standard criteria to assess potential clients for addiction.[13]

The following list represents the typical criteria for addiction when assessing someone for substance use and other addictive disorders, addiction being a maladaptive pattern of behavior, accompanied by psychological and emotional distress, as indicated by one or more of the following criteria:

- You experience a need for increased amounts or novel types of the behavior to achieve the desired effect, or you experience a diminished effect with continued use of the same amount or form of the behavior.
- You experience the characteristic withdrawal symptoms that come with your addictive behaviors, or you perform the behavior or a closely related behavior to relieve or avoid withdrawal symptoms.
- You indulge in more of the behavior or more extreme forms of the behavior, and you spend more time and energy indulging in the behavior than you want or intend to.
- You have an ongoing desire to quit the behavior and have made multiple attempts to stop, cut down, or control the behavior, all to no avail.
- You have given up or reduced your involvement in important projects, tasks, and activities because of the addictive behavior.
- You spend a considerable amount of time and energy performing activities necessary to obtain, indulge in, and recover from the effects of indulging in the addictive behavior.

---

13   See the *DSM-5-TR* for more information.

- You continue indulging in the addictive behavior despite having persistent or recurrent social, interpersonal, occupational, legal, health, or psychological problems that are caused or exacerbated by indulging in the addictive behavior.[14]

You can see how these criteria would apply to someone taking drugs like caffeine, nicotine, alcohol, cannabis, or cocaine. With these addictions, we're led to believe that it's the substance itself that's addictive versus the act of taking the drug. Heroin, for example, is said to be physically addictive because it comes with physical withdrawal symptoms, as do many other drugs. True enough. But the physical addiction, while very real, isn't at the heart of the problem or what makes heroin so addictive. It's the psychological component that's at the heart of all addictive behaviors, including mainlining heroin.

Drug addictions are more accurately defined as behavioral addictions. But typically, addictions are separated into two types: (1) chemical or drug addictions and (2) behavioral addictions. Behavioral addictions are treated by some therapists as second-class citizens, not all that serious, or at least not as serious as drug addictions. But anyone with a shopping, gaming, gambling, eating, or sex addiction knows that's simply not true, not even close. All addictions are behavioral addictions, and those that include taking drugs are not necessarily more serious than those that don't include taking drugs. An addiction is an addiction is an addiction.

This is not to say that all addictions are created equal. Some cause more damage and more suffering than others. But whether drugs are involved isn't always the determining factor. A gambling addiction can just as readily ruin a life as a heroin addiction. It's the *act* of gambling and the *act* of taking heroin and how those behaviors make us *feel* that make them addictive, especially how they make us feel.

Something glaringly absent from the standard criteria for addiction is the word "intoxication," although the diagnostic criteria for alcohol

---

14   Paraphrased from the *DSM-5-TR*.

intoxication is presented separately in the DSM. When we indulge in these behaviors, both those that include ingesting psychoactive drugs and those that don't, we become intoxicated. We find taking drugs or playing video games intoxicating. What exactly do we mean by "intoxicating"? When we drink alcohol, for example, we become intoxicated in one way. We often feel invincible, which is why people who normally would never start throwing punches tend to do just that after one too many drinks. They wildly misjudge their fighting ability, sometimes waking up the next day with a black eye.

Outside of drinking alcohol, calling something intoxicating can simply mean exciting or exhilarating. Visiting the Grand Canyon or bungee jumping would be quite intoxicating in the sense of exhilaration and potentially addictive because we tend to become addicted to that which we find exciting. That's why people become addicted to activities like traveling and bungee jumping.

Buddhists use the word "intoxicating" to describe how we respond to things like our health, youth, lifestyle, and even life itself. For Buddhists, intoxication refers not so much to feeling excited or exhilarated but rather invincible in the way an alcoholic feels invincible while intoxicated. When we're young and healthy, we ignore the fact that it won't always be that way. When we live in a developed country, we take for granted all the benefits we enjoy. We turn the knob, and water comes out. We flick the switch, and the light comes on. Every time! The Buddhists would say we're intoxicated with our good fortune. We take it for granted and feel invincible in the sense of feeling entitled to owning a home, driving a car, and shopping at Whole Foods.

We imagine these are our inalienable rights, and we are intoxicated with them in the sense that we can't see the parameters of our lives. We won't be young forever or always have guaranteed access to what we desire. We know this on one level, of course. But we go about our lives as if we will live forever. We continue to attach ourselves to all manner of impermanent objects, places, people, and activities, ignoring the future consequences of what is often reckless behavior for ourselves, others, and our environment.

What does all this have to do with addiction?

Everything. When you create your vice list, don't just add things like TV, coffee, cheesecake, social media, cigarettes, alcohol, video games, gambling, and pornography. Consider creating a second list, one that includes all the other attachments you never thought of as addictions. For example, consider including how you relate to your age, body, health, socioeconomic status, diet, clothes, transportation, housing, and people who live with you. As any good Buddhist will tell you, you don't own anything or anyone. They're not yours. Moreover, as Buddha teaches, they're not self. There's no permanent essence to any of them.

They're all processes that evolve and pass, briefly existing within the larger process we call the world, which itself represents only a slightly larger process within the infinitely larger process we call the universe. As the Stoics would say, you're not in control of most or maybe even any of it, so stop clinging to all of it. That includes not just the vices you indulge in but also everything with which you're intoxicated, attached to, and addicted to. For most of us, that's everything in our lives. Or as St. Francis of Assisi, a recovering hedonist himself, is said to have put it, learn to "wear the world like a loose garment."

You'll want to understand that addiction, whether to your career or friends, involves being intoxicated, and that always comes to an end. When it does, as it surely will, you'll be left with the consequences of how you behaved while under the influence.

Maybe you got married, had children, and bought a house. Then, to your great surprise, you woke up one day no longer feeling intoxicated, no longer feeling invincible, no longer young, or no longer capable of scoring your drug of choice, whether it be possessions, approval, or success. Maybe your spouse asked for a divorce. Maybe your company forced you to retire. Maybe your kids moved across the country or moved you into a nursing home. You think that will never happen to you, right? But odds are it will. And when it does, you want to be ready to respond with skillfulness and poise, acceptance and equanimity. And that preparation starts here and now.

With the help of the instructions detailed in this book, you'll learn to trade in your intoxications, your addictions, and your attachments for something better, bigger, and brighter. It will be something you can put your trust in and won't turn on you the way your addictions and unhealthy attachments inevitably will if they haven't already.

In step two of the 10 steps of *Breakaway Recovery*, you'll learn how to create a vice list. As you create and review your list, remember that an addiction doesn't have to be full blown to interfere with your success and happiness. Addictions come in degrees, and no degree of addiction is helpful or healthy because all addictions stunt your growth and prevent you from reaching your potential. True, your vices may not kill you, but they will kill your potential. They will kill possibilities that can only be realized if you are playing full out, and you're not playing full out if you're sitting in front of a TV set, eating potato chips, smoking cigarettes, drinking beer, or all the above.

If you're happy spending your time, energy, and money on chips and Netflix, I wish you luck. You're going to need it. I'd encourage you to reconsider. Finish reading this book and follow the instructions. Then read the books recommended in appendix A. If you can get yourself to do that, it's highly likely you'll change your mind about the TV and chips or whatever vices on which you currently spend your time. And you'll be ready to take the first step.

Breakaway Recovery Addiction Criteria

By adopting a much simpler definition of addiction, you can start your journey to a vice-free, self-actualizing life. Here's the *Breakaway Recovery* definition: Addiction is a maladaptive and compulsive pattern of behavior, accompanied by psychological and emotional distress, that prevents you from making the most of yourself and your life.

That's it. That's all there is to it. It implies everything that's included in the *DSM-5*'s standard addiction criteria, but it's all subsumed under this one simple criterion.

As you can see, "addiction" as we're defining it is simpler yet far more inclusive than the official definitions you'll get from the *DSM-5* or American Society of Addiction Medicine, National Institute on Drug Abuse, Substance Abuse and Mental Health Services Administration, National Institute of Mental Health, or World Health Organization's International Classification of Diseases (ICD-11).

This isn't to say these resources don't have plenty to offer. They do. But as we all know, decisions made by committees have their shortcomings, and the decisions made by these committees are no exception. Still, I find that the *DSM*, for example, can be helpful. Its renderings of mental health symptoms do a good job of cataloging and describing the types of suffering Buddha cited in his first noble truth. It wouldn't hurt to become familiar with them. It will help you better understand and alleviate suffering, your own as well as the suffering of the people with whom you live, work, and play.

Now that you have a working definition of addiction—any compulsive behavior that prevents you from making the most of yourself and your life—we'll take a closer look at how addictions operate and what you can do to get beyond them.

4

THE CHAIN THAT BINDS

*The diminutive chains of habit are scarcely ever heavy
enough to be felt, till they are too strong to be broken.*
—Maria Edgeworth, writer, summarizing Samuel Johnson

It's 1977. I'm 24 years old and living the dream as a second-degree black belt and proud owner of a martial arts studio with a Kenpo Karate Jujitsu Kung Fu sign hanging out front. Only this time, the sign is mine. It's hanging on my karate studio, not Rudy Horn's. I practice and teach karate six days a week and go for long runs every day. I absolutely love what I'm doing. It's so good, I sometimes have to pinch myself to make sure I'm not dreaming. As far as I'm concerned, everything is hunky dory, more than hunky dory. Things couldn't be better.

Except for one minor detail—I'm drinking and partying every weekend.

I usually start drinking on Friday nights, continue after teaching on Saturdays and drink again on Sundays. That has me coming in hungover on Saturdays and Mondays, which is the part I'm not so happy with. I do my best to keep this side of my personality hidden from my students. It's as if I'm playing the part of Kwai Chang Caine at work and John Belushi at home.

One of my senior students, a brown belt, comes in every Saturday to work out. We often work out together, and I've gotten to know him pretty well. One time, he left a gram of hash on my desk as a holiday present. We

63

never discussed it, but I was always ready to say I gave it away. He assumed I got high. I pretended I didn't.

One Saturday afternoon, after we finished working out, I closed the school and got ready to head back to Burlington, where I would meet with my drinking buddies and tie one on. As I sat in my car, my student gestured at me from his car. He held up an unlit joint and took an imaginary hit and then stuck it out the window of his car as if to say, "Want to smoke a joint?"

I replied by holding up a banana, peeling it, then holding it out the window of my car as if to say, "Want a bite?"

He laughed, and we both drove away.

That was just one of many incidents that reminded me I wasn't being honest. I wasn't who I was presenting myself to be, and I didn't like the way it made me feel. Still, I went back to Burlington and drank and partied that weekend and for many weekends to come.

The good news is that I eventually found my way out of this dilemma to become the person I am today, drug- and alcohol-free and living what I call the Advancing Life.

The Addiction Chain

In this chapter, we'll take a closer look at addiction, what it is, and how it develops. As anyone who has ever struggled with one knows, addiction is not a simple thing.

Addiction arises for complex reasons that unfold in predictable stages. We can think of those stages as links in a chain, and I'll get into the 20 links that make up what we'll be referring to as the addiction chain. The addiction chain represents the stages in which addictions typically unfold. Examine the list and see if you recognize yourself in these steps. Then read the brief description that follows. In the coming sections, I'll elaborate on these links, including instructions on how to apply strategies that allow you to break each link of the chain and break free from the cycle of addiction.

Don't get hung up on the order of the links. At times, the order may vary, or some links won't always apply to your circumstances. With practice, you'll learn which links apply and how they unfold for you.

What Is Addiction?

Addictive behavior is a futile attempt to find relief from suffering and gain a sense of satisfaction where no such relief or satisfaction exists. Addiction results from compulsive behavior that supplies immediate and sometimes intense yet superficial gratification in the form of relief from discomfort, feelings of pleasure, or both. Addictive behavior may be temporarily rewarding and pleasurable, but it's not fulfilling because it invariably backfires.

Pleasure-producing addictive behavior feels good in the short run but bad in the long run. In the end, the bad feelings outweigh and outlast the good feelings. This is true for all addictive behavior, which is more trouble than it's worth. Addictive behavior promises relief, comfort, pleasure, and satisfaction. The reality is stress, discomfort, displeasure, and a life of chronic dissatisfaction. Addiction—no big surprise—is a lie.

Yet when confronted with their drug of choice, smart people suddenly become, well, reckless. They are reduced to the state of an adolescent in love. Reason flies out the window. Common sense dries up, and emotion takes over. People with addictions have lost sight of reality and become oblivious to the truth of their situation. Down becomes up. Bad becomes good. Wrong becomes right. Addiction, like infatuation, is a kind of hypnosis that mesmerizes its victims, turning them into puppets. By the time they realize the predicament they're in, it's too late. They're hooked and, for the life of them, can't find a way out. Sound familiar?

Keep this in mind as we look at the addiction chain in its entirety. Remember, this is an accurate description of how addiction typically unfolds, though the order and sometimes the links may change. This will give you an overall working map of your destructive behaviors, helping you navigate your way out of the psychological cage called addiction.

These are the links of the chain:

Link 1: Environment

To become addicted, you (the organism) need to be born into an environment and participate in your surroundings. That environment must include something to which you're likely to become addicted. Something in the environment must attract or tempt you with pleasant, rewarding, and reinforcing opportunities. The more appealing those opportunities are, the more likely addiction will occur in your environment. This is environment, the first link in the chain of addiction.

Link 2: Organism

For an addiction to occur, we need an organism capable of becoming addicted. That organism is you and every other sentient being on the planet. If you're alive, and I'll assume that you are because you're reading this book, and if you experience pleasure and pain, comfort and discomfort, then you are an organism capable of becoming addicted. This is organism, the second link in the chain of addiction.

Link 3: Contact

Addiction begins with contact between an organism and its environment. Contact can be physical or mental. When you (the organism) encounter a box of cookies in the aisle of a grocery store (external environment), your addiction gets set in motion. Or you might be out for a walk in the park, not a cookie in sight, when seemingly out of nowhere the thought of eating a cookie comes to mind (internal environment). This is contact, the third link in the chain of addiction.

Link 4: Feeling

Feelings come in three varieties: pleasant, unpleasant, and neutral. When you, the organism in question, experience a pleasant feeling, you're likely to repeat the behavior that sparked it. For example, eating ice cream generally evokes pleasant feelings, which increases the likelihood that you'll do it again—likewise with smoking cigarettes, drinking wine, watching TV, or scrolling through Facebook. This is feeling, the fourth link in the chain of addiction.

Link 5: Cognition

As a human being, you can't help but think about what you experience, including feelings. Once you have an experience, the mental chatter begins: "That was good. I really enjoyed it. I think I'll have another. Hell, it can't hurt to have one more cookie. Can it? No, of course not. Eating one more cookie can't hurt. It's only one more cookie. It's not as if I'm going to eat the whole box." And of course, you end up eating the whole box. This is cognition, the fifth link in the chain of addiction.

Link 6: Craving

Once you see those delicious, mouth-watering chocolate chip cookies, on the store shelf or in your mind's eye, craving takes hold like an itch that demands to be scratched and can't be ignored. Craving is the subjective experience of dopamine flooding your system. Dopamine is the go-get-it neurotransmitter, putting you in hot pursuit of the vice. When you satisfy your craving, your brain's reward center floods your system with happy chemicals. This is craving, the sixth link in the chain of addiction.

Link 7: Preoccupation

Let's say you recently resolved to lose 30 pounds and made a vow to lay off cookies, your favorite snack. But they keep calling to you, inviting you, enticing you, and beguiling you. You've become preoccupied—maybe even a little obsessed—and images of chocolate chip cookies dance in your head. You think, "I must have another cookie." The more you think about it, the more preoccupied you become with whatever it is you crave, and the harder it is to resist. This is preoccupation, the seventh link in the chain of addiction.

Link 8: Agitation

Yes, craving can add excitement to our lives. It can also be seductive, and who doesn't like being seduced, even if it is by a box of cookies? But craving, alas, is a mixed bag. You want the cookies one minute. The next you're not so sure. It will ruin your appetite for dinner. You're trying to cut out refined sugar. You promised yourself no more junk food. You committed to losing 30 pounds. But the cookies keep tempting you.

This back and forth—you want it; you don't want it—is starting to get on your nerves. But still, those cookies would taste *so* good. Ugh! You can't make up your mind. The whole cycle is driving you crazy, and there seems to be only one way to stop it. This is agitation, the eighth link in the chain of addiction.

Link 9: Intention

You tell yourself you can't stand another minute of this torture. You surrender mentally to the cravings and decide to give in to temptation. You devise a plan to indulge. You won't buy the cookies on the store shelf, but when you get home, you'll fire up the oven and bake yourself a batch of homemade chocolate chip cookies. The die is cast. There's no turning back. This is intention, the ninth link in the chain of addiction.

Link 10: Anticipation

Before you finish your walk down the cookie aisle, your mind shifts gears. You go from thinking about the cookies in the abstract to imagining how they'll smell, taste, and feel as you shovel them into your mouth. You can't stop thinking about how good they'll taste; how good it will make you feel to devour those luscious chocolate chip cookies. It's as if you're channeling Homer Simpson. You've not only decided to give in to temptation, but now you're counting down the seconds. This is anticipation, the 10th link in the chain of addiction.

Link 11: Indulgence

It's time. You realize there's no turning back now, so you follow through on your intention. You bake and eat those chocolate chip cookies, just as you knew you would, just as you've done so many times before. As you do, you bask in the warm glow of an addiction being fed. Mmmm … cookies! This is indulgence, the 11th link in the chain of addiction.

Link 12: Intoxication

A profound sense of relief comes over you as you devour those cookies. That's benefit number one. Hot on the heels of that relief comes the second benefit: pleasure. Pleasing sensations permeate your mind and body. You feel *so* good. "This," you tell yourself, "is what makes carrying those extra 30 pounds worth it." You're drunk with delight, and that's all that matters. This is intoxication, the 12th link on the chain of addiction.

Link 13: Reinforcement

Can you see what just happened? By indulging in your guilty pleasure, you were rewarded with relief and pleasure. That reward reinforced the act of eating cookies, ensuring that you'll do it again. Yes, you got rewarded for eating those cookies. But that's not all you got rewarded for. You also got rewarded for breaking your commitment to losing 30 pounds. This is reinforcement, the 13th link in the chain of addiction.

Link 14: Dependence

Do this often enough, and you'll come to rely on the vice in question. Using this example, eating cookies will become your default mode. Feeling bored? Eat a cookie. Need a pick-me-up? Eat a cookie. Having company? Bake some cookies. Now you're channeling the Cookie Monster. This is dependence, the 14th link in the chain of addiction.

Link 15: Tolerance

In time, diminishing returns are bound to set in. You'll need something more, something different, something better to get the relief and pleasure the chocolate chip cookies no longer supply, at least not to the extent they once did. Tolerance means you need more to get the same result. You're eating more but enjoying it less. Where once three cookies did the trick, scratched the itch, and silenced the craving, now it takes six. Soon it will be 40 pounds, not 30, you're trying to lose. This is tolerance, the 15th link in the chain of addiction.

Link 16: Progression

Because of tolerance, you're indulging more frequently and for longer stretches of time. Your addiction progresses and evolves beyond eating cookies. Yes, you're eating more cookies, but that's not all you're doing. You're eating more of other tasty treats as well—ice cream, cake, pie, and pudding, to name just a few. You may even step out into new territory, looking for relief and pleasure in places other than the cookie jar. Maybe now you're having a glass of wine instead of cookies or in addition to cookies. This is Progression, the 16th link in the chain of addiction.

Link 17: Separation

This charade can't go on forever. Tolerance and progression eventually advance to the point where the vice no longer gives any relief, any pleasure. No matter how many cookies you eat, the itch doesn't go away, the craving isn't relieved, the emotional discomfort you try to escape isn't receding. The thrill is gone, and it's not coming back. Or as the Soup Nazi would say, "No soup for you."[15]

At separation, you've reached the end of the line. You may have gone from beer to wine to whiskey, but there's a limit to how much alcohol one beverage contains, and you can only drink so much. Of course, from there,

---

15   *Seinfeld*, episode 116, "The Soup Nazi," directed by Andy Ackerman, written by Spike Feresten, aired November 2, 1995, on NBC.

you could graduate to hard drugs. You could try cocaine, then methamphetamine and heroin. Either way, sooner or later, you'll inevitably run out of places to go. The ladder has a top rung, regardless of your vice. It's time to let go. There's no place left to hide. This is separation, the 17th link in the chain of addiction.

Link 18: Withdrawal

With separation comes withdrawal and withdrawal symptoms. And what do you suppose that means? It's about to get uncomfortable. This is withdrawal, the 18th link in the chain of addiction.

Link 19: Pain

Ouch. Separation and withdrawal hurt, and no amount of ice cream, cake, or cookies can change that. You see, for you, cookies aren't simply a tasty treat. If that were the case, you wouldn't have become addicted to them. For you, cookies serve a higher purpose. They serve as a distraction and coping mechanism. They help you avoid your emotions, or so it seems. What addiction really does is delay the inevitable, and because of tolerance and progression, the inevitable is, well, inevitable. That means it's time to face the pain of whatever you've been trying to escape. Welcome to reality. This is pain, the 19th link in the chain of addiction.

Link 20: Suffering

With separation and withdrawal comes pain, but pain itself isn't the problem. It's just a sensation, a feeling. But when it's a pain you're afraid of, a pain you've been avoiding, running from, or hiding from, that pain quickly becomes suffering, and suffering is the central problem we all face. This is suffering, the 20th link in the chain of addiction.

To be clear, addiction, like everything else, only becomes a problem when it includes suffering. No suffering, no problem. But if you're caught in the grip of addiction, suffering can't be far behind. For most of us, it comes sooner rather than later.

Craving puts us on the path to suffering, and reinforcement and dependence keep us there. To put a stop to it, you'll need to put a stop to your addictions. To do that, you'll need to put a stop to your cravings. And to put a stop to your cravings, you'll need the right skill set, like the one introduced in this book—and you'll need to study, practice, master, and apply it. That's right. There's no quick fix, no magic bullet. Once you accept that, you're on your way.

Suffering Doesn't Wait

There's something else you'll want to consider: Although the addiction chain shows suffering as the last of its 20 links, suffering can show up at any time, and it frequently does, even as soon as the third link. For example, contact with a vice you can't have triggers suffering. Craving, while sometimes exciting, can also be laced with suffering as can preoccupation, agitation, intention, anticipation, indulgence, and even intoxication itself. As you may have figured out, intoxication isn't always all it's cracked up to be. Addiction is a mass of suffering that can and frequently does present itself early in the addiction process.

Take nicotine, for example. Smoking cigarettes will do more than give you cancer. Before it does that, it will yellow your teeth, make you smell like a dirty ashtray, and put you in a state of constant craving, preoccupation, and agitation, all forms of suffering in their own right. Oh, and let's not forget how nonsmokers will judge you, and all the while you, too, are thinking less of yourself.

The Many Flavors of Addiction

It's possible that you're still eating cookies and feeling relief and pleasure without progressing to suffering. You eat more cookies than you'd like, and you've gained some extra weight, but hey, it's only 10 or 20 pounds, and you can live with that. You figure it's worth it. It may not be ideal, but you can't have everything. So, you'll stick with the cookies and live with the extra weight.

While admittedly not a good habit, you reason, it's certainly not an addiction. Addictions, after all, are in large part defined by tolerance, progression, and withdrawal. If you don't have any of these, then you don't have an addiction, right?

Wrong.

Not every addiction leads to tolerance, progression, and withdrawal, but all addictions include the other links. You're indulging in a vice (link 11), for example, and no amount of vice is good for you. You're still dependent on the vice (link 14), and it's not a healthy dependence. And although there may be no separation (link 17) and no withdrawal (link 18), you will experience the pain (link 19) and suffering (link 20) that comes with relying on unwholesome and unhealthy behaviors. These vices find their way into your body and mind, and they aren't good for either one.

Up to this point, you've learned how to identify and understand your addiction. The rest of the book will show you how to eliminate and replace those nasty varmints—once and for all!

5

THE STEPS WE TOOK

The journey of a thousand miles begins with one step.
—attributed to Lao Tzu, Chinese philosopher

It's 1978, and I'm 25 years old. I've been practicing martial arts since 1973 and teaching since 1975. I also run consistently six days a week. Often when I go into a local store, the cashier says, "Oh, you're the guy I see running all over town." I was Forrest Gump before Forrest Gump, an ultramarathoner before there was such a thing.

As we've seen, I also lead a double life. I presented myself as a disciplined Shaolin monk of sorts to my karate students. But on weekends, I was still clubbing, drinking, and whooping it up. I'd often come back to the studio on Mondays with a hangover and lock myself in my office, pretending I was meditating. In reality, I was trying to recover before I had to teach.

Then something happened. After a night of particularly heavy drinking and cocaine use, I woke up paralyzed. I tried to get out of bed but couldn't. As I lay there, I realized it was because of the alcohol and drugs.

"God, I don't know if you can hear me. I don't even know if you exist. But I have to tell someone, and there's no one else around. So, here it is," I said aloud. "I will never drink again. I'm done. And I'm not asking you to cure me. I know I don't deserve it. I did this to myself."

I felt in my heart that I would recover; and gratefully, over the next few weeks, my ability to move gradually returned until I was back to normal and began my new sober adventure.

I had tried to quit drinking several times before, but this time, something felt different. I knew as I made the declaration that it was true. I would never drink or take any other recreational drugs again. And I haven't. Nor have I wanted to. I've never even been tempted, never had an urge or a craving. That was more than *45* years ago.

Since that fateful day, I've given up a total of 52 vices. I've made it a tradition to give up another vice every September 1, which I will continue to do until I have no more vices left. I encourage you to set the same goal— to become and remain vice-free.

When the conflict between the person I wanted to be and the person I had become became painful enough, I made a change for the better. I wanted to be the person I was presenting myself as to my karate students. That final hangover that left me temporarily paralyzed finally convinced me that drinking was something I no longer wanted to do, so I stopped. Convincing myself to abandon my other vices that didn't come with such obvious drawbacks took something else. Over time, I developed that "something else" and succeeded in using it. That something else is the breakaway recovery method, and I've been teaching it to my clients ever since.

Now I'm introducing it to you in this book so that you, too, can become and remain vice-free. The 10 steps will put you on the path to success and happiness—if you follow them closely.

Breakaway Recovery: **The Steps You'll Take**

It's time to introduce you to the steps you'll take to overcome your addictive behaviors. This section introduces you to the steps, and the rest of the book shows you how to take them. These steps are the runway for your flight to a new life. If you follow these simple (but not always easy) instructions, along with the additional instructions detailed in the remainder of the book, success is all but sure to follow.

First, read through the 10 steps to get an idea of how they work and what you'll be doing. Then come back and start the process. These instructions, together with the instructions in the rest of the book, give you everything you need to master the 10 steps. I strongly suggest you read through the rest of the book first before taking action so you're better prepared to begin.

These steps are meant to be taken and ideally completed so you don't have to refer to them again and again. Taking them will bring you to a new domain, not one merely of concepts and ideas but a domain of *behavioral* transformation. If you follow the steps thoroughly, you'll never have to look back. Read them carefully. Follow them closely. Do as they say, and they will bring you to your point of departure, leaving you free of your bad habits, vices, addictions, and unhealthy attachments—and ready to move on to bigger and better things.

The 10 Steps of *Breakaway Recovery*

Step 1

Acknowledge that you are indulging in a series of addictive behaviors.

Step 2

Make a list of these behaviors and arrange the list in the order you plan to renounce them.

Step 3

Resolve to abandon the entire range of these self-sabotaging behaviors.

Step 4

Set a quit date for the first behavior on the list, and mark this day on your calendar.

Step 5

Mobilize yourself for success by highlighting the drawbacks of indulging and the benefits of abstaining.

Step 6

When your quit date arrives, stop indulging in the addictive behavior.

Step 7

If at any time you feel tempted to resume the addictive behavior, counter the temptation using one or more of the breakaway recovery strategies, tools, or techniques.

Step 8

If for any reason, you break your commitment to abstaining from the addictive behavior, set another quit date and resume following the above steps until you have permanently eliminated it from your list.

Step 9

Continue to renounce each item on your list using the steps outlined above until you have eliminated the entire range of your addictive behaviors.

Step 10

Share the message of vice-free living by helping others identify and eliminate their own addictive behaviors.

AA uses the word "recovery" to describe what happens when an alcoholic stops drinking. The proposed disease of alcoholism goes into remission, and the alcoholic gets better. For AA, "recovery" is a medical term related to the disease of alcoholism. I, too, use the term "recovery" but not in the same way. I use it to mean recovering lost potential.

Although I ask you to maintain that alcoholism is not a disease, I want you to see it as potential that has been squandered on indulging in and feeding vices. It's that lost potential, along with lost opportunities, that you recover when you abandon your vices. *Breakaway Recovery* shows you, step-by-step, how to recover, develop, and reach the upper limits of that lost potential. Yes, you can get it back, certainly some of it and maybe all of it. You'll also learn to recognize and seize new opportunities that may well turn out to be even more promising than the ones you missed.

Now let's take a closer look at the 10 steps that make up the heart of what some might say is a radical approach to becoming and remaining vice-free.

Step 1

Acknowledge that you are indulging in a series of addictive behaviors.

Like the first of AA's 12 steps, we start by acknowledging the problem. We have an addiction, and if we're being honest about it, more than one. If you have a human brain attached to a human body, then you're naturally prone to developing addictive behaviors. It's just the way we evolved and how natural selection built us. You're not to blame if you've become addicted to virtually every pleasure-producing thing in sight. You've inherited this addictive tendency from your ancestors. Nevertheless, it is your responsibility to acknowledge it, address it, and ultimately override it. No one can do it for you, although some of us can help.

We hesitate to acknowledge our addictive behaviors for numerous reasons, not the least of which is that we don't want to stop. We enjoy our morning cigarette, cup of coffee, or second martini, but these are addictive behaviors we use to avoid or escape from our real problem. If you believe drinking alcohol is your only problem, or even your main problem, see what happens when you try to quit. You'll start guzzling instead of sipping your morning coffee, and the cup quickly turns into a pot.

That's right. Give up alcohol, and you'll start drinking coffee by the pot. And that pack-a-day cigarette habit? If you give up alcohol, make it two packs. If you're like most of us, you use a range of these addictive behaviors to calm your nerves, quiet the mental chatter in your mind, and help you escape the discomfort that comes with being human. That discomfort is the real problem—and the only problem.

Step one is about admitting this all-but-unavoidable fact of life: We are a nation of addicts, if not a species of addicts. To be human, especially to be human living in a modern, developed country, is to be engaged in a series of addictive behaviors, often from the moment we wake up until the moment we go to sleep. If you think chugging whiskey, smoking crack, or mainlining heroin are the only real addictions, think again. Anything used to excess or that distracts you from or undermines your success and happiness is an addictive behavior. If what you're doing makes you less successful and less happy, if it blocks you from making the most of yourself and your life and reaching your full potential, classify that as an addictive behavior.

Again, it's not just mainlining heroin, smoking crack, or drinking whiskey. Things like watching sports and compulsively checking email or the weather also belong on your list. Not all of these are always engaged in addictively. You can use your smartphone responsibly. You can watch YouTube videos selectively. But you probably don't. More likely, you do some, most, or all the above activities to avoid or escape the suffering that comes with what's going on in your mind.

The point is we're inundated with distractions and temptations that block the path to success and happiness in front of us. Step one asks you to acknowledge this fact and admit that you, too, like so many of us, indulge in a long list of addictive behaviors that squash your potential, and leave you a mere shell of the person you could be. And that is the person you can be if you commit to identifying and eliminating these potential-killing habits.

Do you acknowledge that you indulge in a series of addictive behaviors? Is it obvious or not? If not, and you're not sure it's true for you, then it's time to do some research. Spend the next week or two examining your behavior. Notice what you do each day, and ask yourself why you do it. If you're not sure if it's an addiction or not, try going without it. Shut the TV off for a week and see how that goes. Give up drinking coffee for a week and see what happens. How does that compare to giving up broccoli for a week?

You'll notice, as you continue experimenting, that certain activities are harder to do without than others and not because you need them to survive. I'm not asking you to go without water or food, just soda and cookies. Forgo the salty french fries with ketchup and have a baked sweet potato instead—plain, no butter, no salt, no spices. How do you feel? Hell, you may not even have to do it. Just thinking about doing it may trigger a panic attack. "Give up french fries and ketchup? Give up butter and jelly on my toast? Are you crazy? Have you lost your mind?" The same can be said for watching and reading the news. Are you a news junkie? Give it up for a month or even just a week to find out.

Once you realize you really are addicted to these types of behaviors, it's time to generate the list. In step 2, you'll spend as much time as it takes to catalog all the things you do that aren't in your best interest over the long term, or even in the short term. Include the many things you do to avoid facing reality, doing the hard work of making the most of yourself and your life, including everything that keeps you stuck in mediocrity and unable to sit peacefully alone in a room with nothing but your thoughts. Ask yourself, "Why can't I do that?" It's often because your thoughts are a never-ending stream of negativity. Not always. Not all of them. But many of them, much of the time. It's these thoughts and the toxic emotions that accompany them that drive you to drink coffee, smoke cigarettes, read romance novels, or do whatever it is you do to shut off the mental chatter.

Once you've acknowledged that you indeed indulge in a series of addictive behaviors, it's time to move on to step 2. Congratulations! You're on your way. Good things are in store.

Step 2

Make a list of these behaviors and arrange the list in the order you plan to renounce them.

If you are truly addicted to something, you can no more say no to your cravings than a drowning person can say no to a breath of fresh air. Of course, both scenarios are possible but highly unlikely. As far as you're concerned, you simply can't resist. Refusing the siren call of your favorite vice is out of the question, even when you know of its dangers. If the object of your addiction is available, there's just no two ways about it. You're going to indulge. As far as you can tell, there's no alternative.

True, if someone holds a gun to your head, you'll suddenly find it within your power to refuse. But remove the gun, and the desire to indulge overtakes you again, and you're off to the races or the pub or the crack house or wherever the case may be. Just saying no doesn't work … unless you know *why* saying no is a better option than saying yes. And that is the simple secret of breaking free from any addiction. You must have the right reason or reasons to say no. Once you have those reasons, saying no will become automatic, just as saying yes is automatic now. You'll discover those reasons when we get to step 5.

It's common for those with a serious addiction to enter treatment or a 12-step program for help with their specific addiction. The addiction could be anything. There's a problem, however, with focusing exclusively on one main addictive behavior, even a serious, life-threatening behavior like smoking cigarettes, drinking alcohol, or mainlining heroin. Yes, by all means, if you have such an addiction, put it first on your list. But once you've freed yourself from its deadly grip, don't stop there. Your other addictive behaviors, the ones you imagine are harmless or relatively harmless, aren't.

Going from drinking a six-pack of beer to drinking a pot of coffee may be an improvement. It may even be a big improvement. But you're still just kicking the can down the road with these types of substitute addictions, trading one vice for another. It's not uncommon to attend an AA meeting and see members outside guzzling coffee and scarfing down donuts while sucking on cigarettes. Sure, you've eliminated your alcohol addiction. Great! But you're still not sober, at least not as we're defining it here. Being sober means being vice-free, not just alcohol- or drug-free.

If you've been able to give up alcohol or hard drugs, great! That's a terrific start. I don't want to minimize it. Some vices are more harmful than others. Drinking whiskey, smoking crack, or mainlining heroin are all worse than drinking coffee. But still, no vice is a good vice. Or to put it another way, the only good vice is a former vice. By all means, put those killer vices at the top of your list. But if you're trading beer for coffee, you're simply trading one vice for another. Yes, a pot of coffee is better than a six-pack of beer, but you can do even better. Trade in that coffee for a vegetable smoothie.

Put the pot of coffee on your list along with all your other vices, large and small, major and minor, and adopt the motto: A vice is a vice is a vice.

Contrary to popular opinion, there's no such thing as a harmless vice. Less harmful? Granted. But still not harmless.

Now, let's talk about how to create that list.

You can start by brainstorming a list of possible vices. I organized my list into four categories: drugs, entertainment, food, and sex. Then I arranged the items in each category in the order I planned to renounce them. It didn't always work out the way I planned, so I simply updated the list to reflect the reality of when I renounced each item in a particular category. My list, as you'll soon see, shows the order in which I eliminated each item by category. On the list, rock radio comes before strip joints. But I gave up going to strip joints before I gave up listening to rock radio. I allowed myself to jump from one category to another, checking off each vice as I went along.

Alternatively, you can create a separate list for each of your categories, if you decide to use categories. You can organize your vices the way I did or simply list them in the order you plan to renounce them, ignoring how each vice relates to the others. In other words, you don't need categories, just a list. Come up with a system that works for you.

For my drug list, the order you see is pretty much the order I eliminated them, one at a time, except for barbiturates, amphetamines, and cocaine, which I jettisoned all at once. I gave up all booze at once, including beer, wine, and hard liquor, listing it together as alcohol. For the non-alcoholic beverages, I eliminated soft drinks first, then later I eliminated coffee, tea, and hot chocolate at the same time. As far as sweets go, candy went first. Then a little later, all the others in one go.

I tried allowing myself to have pumpkin pie once a year on Thanksgiving. As you can imagine, that didn't work out so well. The second year, I ended up eating three pies—not three pieces, mind you, three whole pies. I also ate chips for a while, but eventually let that go because of the salt and because I actually couldn't eat just one chip, only one full bag. And of course, I'm happy to be rid of it all. Remember, though, the happiness that comes with being rid of a vice only comes once indulging is no longer an option and when you know it's no longer something you'd consider doing. Then the struggle is over, and you can relax and enjoy yourself without constantly fighting off urges and cravings.

People tend to think eating junk food, smoking pot, or watching porn makes them happy. It doesn't. It can't. If you pay attention to the whole process (before, during, and after), you'll find that it's nothing but a mass of suffering. If you can't yet see the suffering, that's because you've never experienced happiness, at least not authentic happiness. You simply have nothing to compare your addictive pleasures to. It's all you know. Like all people trapped in addiction, you wouldn't know happiness if it bit you. That's okay. In future chapters, we'll address the issue of happiness, teaching you how to recognize it, how to generate it, and how to make it your mainstay.

Now, take out your journal or open your laptop and begin brainstorming your list. The list should include anything you do to distract yourself or drown out the worried, chattering voice in your head and the emotional turmoil that comes with it. Addiction, it turns out, isn't as much about chasing pleasure as it is about escaping pain.

As we know, nature abhors a vacuum. For many of us, it's helpful to make two lists: one list of addictive behaviors we're determined to eliminate and another list of the alternative behaviors with which we chose to replace them. You not only want to eliminate your bad habits, but you also want to replace them with much better ones, which are the key to your success. This is especially true for the supernormal stimuli to which you've been addicted. These vices have your brain's pleasure center lighting up like a Christmas tree every time you indulge. And as you know, this kind of pleasure isn't easy to resist. But as you also know, and know only too well, the price you pay for that pleasure is high, too high, far too high.

Yes, indulging feels good, but not for long. When it ends, payment comes due, and that payment isn't an amount you can afford. And, metaphorically speaking, when the bill collector comes calling, it won't be a polite or patient one. Your collector will more likely resemble a limb-breaking enforcer from *The Godfather* or *The Sopranos*. Before it comes to that, if it hasn't already, let's get those bills paid. And we'll start by cutting up our credit cards and giving up our spending sprees—literally for some, metaphorically for others.

Once you've made your lists, it's time to move on to step 3. But first, take a look at the example list below:

Vice List

- ✓ Cigarettes
- ✓ LSD
- ✓ Benzodiazepines
- ✓ Barbiturates
- ✓ Amphetamines
- ✓ Cocaine
- ✓ Marijuana
- ✓ Alcohol
- ✓ Cruising and hanging
- ✓ Clubs and bars
- ✓ Harvard Square
- ✓ Rock music
- ✓ Television
- ✓ Social media
- ✓ Mainstream media
- ✓ Soft drinks
- ✓ Coffee
- ✓ Tea
- ✓ Hot chocolate
- ✓ Candy
- ✓ Donuts
- ✓ Brownies
- ✓ Fudge
- ✓ Cake
- ✓ Ice cream
- ✓ Pastry
- ✓ Pudding
- ✓ Cookies
- ✓ Pie
- ✓ Chips
- ✓ Fast food
- ✓ Table sugar
- ✓ Table salt
- ✓ Red meat
- ✓ Poultry
- ✓ Fish
- ✓ Dairy
- ✓ Eggs
- ✓ Overeating
- ✓ Strip joints
- ✓ Strippers
- ✓ Casual sex
- ✓ Porn
- ✓ Fapping
- ✓ Racy movies
- ✓ Eye candy
- ✓ Lusting
- ✓ Flirting
- ✓ Fantasizing
- ✓ Romantic infatuation
- ✓ Falling in love
- ✓ Being in love

Step 3

Resolve to abandon the entire range of these self-sabotaging behaviors.

People are hardwired to develop addictions. We're innately subject to craving and attaching. We instinctively foster and nurture our addictions. We're inherently subject to desire—that is, to wanting things, typically things that make us feel good. Yet our desires can be weakened and even eliminated. Even thirst and hunger are malleable. You're not stuck with your current addictions, whatever they may be.

Step 3 involves making a commitment to renounce not just one or two of your many addictive behaviors, the most troubling or worrisome habits, but all of them, every last one. Major or minor, if you're a serious quitter, they must all go. Decide that you'll eliminate your addictive behaviors and then make a formal commitment to do it. "Deciding" means cutting off all other options, especially the option to opt out of what it is you've decided to do. Once the decision has been made, you'll commit to doing whatever is necessary to make it happen, come rain or shine. To lock in your commitment, it helps to make a formal pledge. This is a promise you make to yourself and can't break—a promise you *won't* break. Once you're truly committed, you'll naturally become dedicated in both heart and mind to making your decision a reality, no matter what that entails.

This decision to abandon your vices can feel daunting at first. This reluctance comes from a failure to see things clearly as they are, not as you imagine them to be. You imagine you're giving up something of value. You're not. True, you'll be giving up a certain amount of pleasure, but it's a type of pleasure that inevitably turns into its opposite. The better you feel now, the worse you'll feel later. That's how addictions work—all of them. The ones that begin with a little pleasure end in a little pain. The ones that begin with lots of pleasure end in lots of pain. The better the addictive behavior feels now, the worse it will feel later.

Fortunately, there's a way around this. Give up your vices—all of them! Does that sound too extreme? It might. But once you learn to see your vices for what they are, letting them go will be easy. As this step points out, your vices are nothing more than self-sabotaging behaviors, leading you to a mass of suffering if you continue surrendering to their seductive provocations. Why on earth would you hesitate to be done with them? Only because you can't quite see the truth of the matter. But don't worry. You'll get there.

It's important you realize that you are primarily responsible for becoming addicted so that you can get yourself unaddicted. True, you had plenty of help. You grew up surrounded by people who encouraged your addictive behavior in one way or another. Now, you'll get unaddicted with plenty of encouragement and help from this book. But encouragement or not, it's up to you to free yourself. No one can do it for you. Those of us who have already done it can and will show you the path. Once we do, it's up to you to follow it. Have you taken step 1? Have you owned up to your addictive behaviors? Have you taken step 2? Have you made a list of your vices? Have you taken this third step? Have you resolved to abandon those addictive behaviors? If not, now is the time to do it. Go back to steps 1, 2, and 3, and follow the instructions.

Once you've completed these three steps, it will be time to move on to step 4—toward a life of freedom and opportunity.

Step 4

Set a quit date for the first behavior on your list, and mark this day on your calendar.

Before you make that commitment and set that date, let's make sure you're ready. If not, let's estimate how much time you'll likely need to get ready. You want to give yourself the best chance of succeeding once you start. To determine your degree of readiness and where you are on your path of behavioral change, we'll use a six-phase model called the stages of change, first developed by psychologists James Prochaska and Carlo

DiClemente in 1983.[16] (I added the third stage.) These are the stages of change:

1. Precontemplation
2. Contemplation
3. Determination
4. Preparation
5. Action
6. Maintenance
7. Conclusion or relapse

If you've made it this far, you're beyond the precontemplation and contemplation stages. Those in the precontemplation stage don't know they have a problem and haven't given it any thought. Or if they have, they've decided they don't have a problem. You've not only thought about quitting, but you've also resolved to do so. Those in the contemplation stage are considering whether their involvement with the vice in question is a problem or not.

You've made it through the first three steps of *Breakaway Recovery*, which puts you in the determination stage. That means you've acknowledged that you have a problem, you've created a list of your addictive behaviors, and you've resolved to renounce them. You're ready for the preparation stage.

Before setting the actual quit date, review step 5 of breakaway recovery. This step shows you more about how to prepare yourself to quit the addictive behavior. Estimate how much time you think you'll need, but this doesn't have to be exact. In fact, there's no way for you to know how long it will take, nor is it necessary. The only way to truly know if you're ready is to try and see what happens. At step 6, you'll make the attempt. If you fail, step 8 tells you what to do. At the same time, its message is "If at first

---

16　James O. Prochaska and Carlo C. DiClemente, "Stages and Processes of Self-Change of Smoking: Toward an Integrative Model of Change," *Journal of Consulting and Clinical Psychology*, 51, no. 3 (1983), 390–395, https://doi.org/10.1037/0022-006X.51.3.390.

you don't succeed, try, try again." As you'll see, failure is simply a part of the process. Don't worry about it. You'll learn how to turn your failures to your advantage.

Now, make your best guess at how long you'll need to get ready, then pick a date and mark it on your calendar. When your quit date is chosen, it's time to move on to step 5.

Step 5

Mobilize yourself for success by highlighting the drawbacks of indulging in the addictive behavior and the benefits of renouncing it.

Think of step 5 as going to the gym. The gym is where you train for the fight. It's here you prepare yourself to step into the ring with your addiction. There are multiple ways to do this. Here are six key strategies:

Strategy 1

When battling your addictions, keep in mind that you're at war with the addiction, not yourself. It's easy to forget this and get caught up in blaming yourself for doing what natural selection and your environment conditioned you to do and what any other *Homo sapiens* would do, given the same circumstances. You're still responsible for overcoming your addictions. But when you try and fail, castigating yourself is counterproductive. You're only human. You have limitations. Sometimes those limitations will prevent you from succeeding. It comes with the territory.

When it comes to battling your addictions, accept that you won't win every battle and know that this is irrelevant, provided you keep doing as instructed. Regardless of how many times you try and fail (and because you're new at this, you will initially fail), you'll eventually succeed if you keep at it. Those first failures are simply steps along the path to success. Don't resist them. Don't resent them. Don't regret them. Welcome them. That's right—embrace them. They are unavoidable and indispensable components of the process. Be grateful for every relapse and the lessons they teach you. Each brings you closer to success.

A few of your vices will go down without a fight. Some will give you a run for your money. Others will fight to the death. A heroin addiction, for example, is out to kill you. It wants you dead. Not literally, of course—heroin isn't plotting against you—but your use of it could very likely end in your death. With each type of vice, whether it's an annoying habit like biting your nails or a killer drug addiction, you have to be willing to take on that challenge and do whatever it takes to succeed. That includes studying, practicing, and applying the various strategies detailed in this book.

Strategy 2

Start by identifying what you're missing out on when you choose to indulge in your addictive behaviors. Start keeping track of how much time you spend on a particular vice. This can be a real eye-opener. My guess is you'll be surprised, if not shocked, at how much time you're wasting and could be spending on something worthwhile. Then consider what that something else might be.

What could you do instead of watching TV? One of my clients lamented that she could have earned a PhD in the time she spent chasing drugs. You may not be addicted to drugs, but maybe you haven't gotten around to writing that book you've set your heart on because you're a social media addict, and that nonsense keeps you from writing your book.

According to Statista, the average person watches three hours of TV a day.[17] So, let's say your vice is watching TV. If you watch three hours of TV a day, that adds up to 21 hours a week. What could you do with 21 hours a week? Your addictive behavior is costing you a lot.

Now, imagine the benefits of dropping that behavior and replacing it with something better that you actually care about, that you've always wanted to do but didn't think you had the time. Guess what? You do have the time, just as soon as you drop that addictive behavior, whatever that behavior is for you.

---

17   Julia Stoll, "Average Daily Time Spent Watching TV per Capita in the United States from 2009 to 2022, by Age Group," Statista, September 1, 2023, https://www.statista.com/statistics/411775/average-daily-time-watching-tv-us-by-age/.

Strategy 3

As you go about your day, you'll face many choices. But there will always be only two main categories: (1) healthy options and (2) unhealthy options.

When considering what to do, especially if you catch yourself considering an unhealthy option, a vice-related option, stop and think. Consider the drawbacks and the benefit of indulging compared to choosing a healthy alternative. You can sit on the couch and play video games all night. Or you can go for a run, read a good book, study for a test, or call a friend. Good options always exist, just as bad ones do.

Step 5 is when you develop the habit of weighing your options, reviewing your vice and virtue lists, and contemplating the drawbacks of indulging in the vice. You also identify healthy alternatives that will lead you up from the basement of addiction and out into the light of a brand-new day, a brand-new life, and a brand-new you.

Strategy 4

If you understood the drawbacks of addictive behaviors, that would be enough to stop you from indulging. But we humans are clever creatures, and we're inexplicably good at deceiving ourselves. When we're under the influence of cravings and urges, we block out the facts. We conveniently forget how bad indulging ourselves gets—how uncomfortable, how painful, and how damaging. We must remind ourselves. We must look back and identify the painful and destructive consequences of our past addictive behaviors. Then we must use consequential thinking to predict the future and envision the pain and destruction that are sure to come if we continue on as we are.

These consequences come with even seemingly harmless vices. But when we're experiencing urges and cravings, we won't always want to remember the painful consequences of indulging. We'll want to indulge and experience the pleasant feelings that come with indulging, so we'll push the painful memories out of our minds. This means you'll have to routinely review the negative aspects of indulging in your vice over an extended period of time if that's what it takes. This is often the only way we can get it through our thick skulls that addictive behavior isn't worth the trouble that comes with it! Once you not only understand it intellectually but also know it in your heart of hearts, you'll no longer have to resist your vices. You'll find them to be repulsive.

Strategy 5

Rehearsing the painful consequences of indulging is only half the battle. Fortunately, the other half is about thinking ahead to pleasure. After getting clear about the drawbacks of indulging, you'll want to convince yourself that abstinence has benefits that will match and then exceed the benefits you get from indulging in a vice. Some of those benefits will come naturally as a result of renouncing the vice. But for some of you, it will take something more.

If you're dealing with a potent vice that falls into the category of supernormal stimulus and provides you with extreme relief and pleasure, or if it's a vice you've been relying on for some time, it helps to replace that vice with something equally rewarding, reinforcing, and compelling. The substitute behavior must be capable of competing with the vice.

This could amount to something as radical as figuring out your life's purpose. Once you decide what that is, you'll need a deep conviction in the urgency, importance, and timeliness of your purpose leaving no room for thinking about, let alone indulging in, your addictive behaviors.

Can you see why something of this magnitude might be what you need? If your vice amounts to a supernormal stimulus, that includes things like drugs, pornography, and anything else that lights up your pleasure centers in unhealthy ways. To be successful in eclipsing your addiction, you'll need something equally or even more appealing than the supernormal stimulus you're currently addicted to.

More on what that something is coming up shortly.

Strategy 6

This strategy involves taking time to really think about things. As soon as you feel yourself tempted by a vice, apply one or more of the *Breakaway Recovery* addiction busters (introduced shortly) and take notes. Write down your thoughts in your reframe journal (also coming up). Each time you review what you've written, you'll gain new insights. Jot them down. Keep a written record of your insights, and review and update them frequently. This will go a long way in uprooting your cravings and ultimately freeing you from your addictions. We'll cover exactly how to do this when we get to the section on how to keep a reframe journal.

You'll find that what works for overcoming one vice won't necessarily work with another. Different strategies work with different vices. The strategies that helped you overcome your cigarette addiction, for example, may not help with your porn addiction. If you're struggling with a porn addiction, it's important to know what you're up against. A porn addiction starts with your body's primitive reproductive system. You're hardwired to crave sex, which is designed to be highly pleasurable. You may have noticed.

In addition to your body's hardwired reproductive system, you have a learning history. Let's call that your software. This means you're hardwired to crave sex in general, and you're programmed to crave it in specific ways unique to what you learned as you grew up. Giving up pornography will be challenging, to say the least. You'll have to experiment with the various strategies you learn and will continue to learn as you make your way through this book.

Once you understand these strategies and are confident you can apply them, along with completing the other four *Breakaway Recovery* steps, it's time to move on to step 6. Are you ready to renounce the next vice on your list? If not, continue working on earlier strategies. If so, dig in. (A little reminder—be sure to read the book through once before taking any action.)

Step 6

When your quit date arrives, stop indulging in the addictive behavior.

Now that your quit date has arrived, maybe you think you're not quite ready to give up the vice in question. You tell yourself it's only a matter of time before you will be. You're almost there, almost ready to let it go. It won't be long. You can feel it. For now, you'll sit tight and go with the flow until you decide you are ready.

Hooey! That's addiction talking. If you're like most of us, you've been saying that for as long as you can remember. You've been trying to beat this vice for years, maybe decades. Count them. How long has it been? Five months? Five years? Five decades? All the while, you've been telling yourself that you'll quit but not today, that you'll give it up soon or that you're not quite ready. You continue telling yourself the same old story as you indulge.

I'm here to tell you that you *are* ready, and today is the day. It's the date you committed to and marked on your calendar. The only day you can't do it is someday, because someday is the one day that never comes. No wait, my mistake. There's one other day you can't do it: tomorrow. You can't do it someday, and you can't do it tomorrow. You can only do it today.

Putting it off is the only thing stopping you from stopping. Oops, another oversight! There's one more thing that can prevent you from breaking free from this wretched vice, and that's telling yourself, "Someday, maybe …," as in, "Someday, maybe I'll quit if everything goes well (or I'm in the right mood, having a good day, or feeling lucky, or the stars are lined up just right), then maybe, just maybe, I'll quit." Now it's no longer someday, which was bad enough. Now it's someday maybe. You tell yourself, "Someday, maybe I'll break this self-defeating habit. When that day arrives, that magical day called someday maybe, the miracle will happen. I'll just wait for that special day to arrive. Then the struggle will be over, and I'll finally be free."

But now you know that's not how it works, and I'll bet you already knew it. You didn't need me to tell you, just to remind you. This is another habit you'll need to put on your vice list, the habit of putting things off until someday maybe. There's no such day as someday maybe, and there's no such thing as magic or quick fixes. There's only knowledge, determination, discipline, and grit. There's only your willingness to do whatever it takes to abandon your addictive behaviors, starting with the vice you decided to give up starting today.

Stop indulging and use step 7 to thwart any temptations you encounter. If worse comes to worst, use step 8 to deal with a relapse. Otherwise, you're ready to skip ahead to step 9.

Step 7

If at any time you feel tempted to resume the addictive behavior, counter the temptation using one or more of the *Breakaway Recovery* strategies, tools, or techniques.

Our intention is to remain free from the grip of the vice. Some of us will lose interest in the vice by the time we make it through the first three steps or sooner. This was true for me when I quit drinking alcohol. I lost all interest in drinking because the drawbacks were painfully clear, and I was no longer willing to tolerate them. I no more wanted to drink a glass of beer or wine than a glass of urine. In fact, if someone held a gun to my head and said I had to drink one or the other or be shot in the head, I'd choose to drink the urine.

To say I lost my taste for drinking alcohol is an understatement. I loathed the very thought of it—and not just the hangovers or the other nasty consequences. When I thought about getting a buzz on, the very thing that kept me hooked for all those years, it no longer held any appeal for me. Everything about drinking, from the thought of feeling intoxicated and enduring another hangover to getting another DUI, provided all the motivation I needed to give up the nasty habit.

It's great when that happens, but it doesn't always work that way. I still find other vices on my list attractive, so I have to deal with temptation when it strikes. For step 7, start by visualizing the vice itself as nothing more than a form of bait placed inside a cage. To get it, you have to step into the cage and grab it, but once you do, the door slams shut and traps you in the cage. You got the bait, the thing you thought you wanted, but now you're trapped in a cage of addiction. The bait will soon run out, and you'll be stuck inside with nothing but regret, alone and wishing you were somewhere else, anywhere else. *Don't take the bait!* It's never worth it. You'll always be worse off than if you had left it alone.

What do you get from indulging in the vice you've committed to renouncing? A few minutes of relief so fleeting that you end up crawling back, begging for more, days, hours, or even minutes later? Or do you do it for the tiny bit of pleasure you get, which doesn't quite satisfy or do what it used to do? You take a little more, hoping this time will be different.

Maybe you're in an even tougher spot. Maybe the vice delivers lots of relief and lots of pleasure. Maybe it does just what you want it to. Maybe you spend hours lost in the addiction, oblivious to the world around you, freed from your problems and responsibilities. Besides, you're showing up for work. You're paying your bills. You're taking care of business. That may be true, but the rest of the time, you're lost in the world of *Grand Theft Auto V*, oblivious to what's going on around you and opportunities in the real world passing you by. You've learned to ignore those missed opportunities because thinking about them would be too painful.

Still, in the back of your mind, you know that you're missing out on what's most important. Maybe you have a job but not a career. Maybe you have a career but not a mission. Maybe you have a wife and children who barely see you. Underneath it all, you know there's something better and real that you're sacrificing for the superficial relief and pleasure you get from your addictive behaviors. You've traded a life of meaning and purpose for a cheap thrill.

Well, not anymore! Today, all that changes. Today is the day you've chosen to fight back. Today is the day you set as your quit date—not tomorrow, not someday, and not someday maybe. Today, no matter what! Not if all goes well, not if you're in the right mood, not if you're having a good day, not if you're feeling up to it, and not if you're finally ready. Ready or not, it's time to declare war on this vice.

Here's the deal: You're committing to taking out this once-unstoppable addiction once and for all, first by beating it into submission, then by knocking it unconscious, and finally by snuffing it out of existence, mercifully putting it out of its misery. Every time you get an urge to indulge in the vice, you'll respond with the full force of the *Breakaway Recovery* strategies you're learning about in this book.

If you get an urge to indulge, think about how addiction and vice took your formative years from you and why you're determined to prevent that from ever happening again. Think about why you won't let this addiction cheat you out of your current education opportunities the way it cheated you out of your earlier education, if that's what happened to you. If you get an urge while socializing, think about how your early addictions damaged and, in some cases, destroyed your relationships. Consider the strain it put on those relationships and the suffering it caused your family and how it prevented you from forming new and healthier relationships that would have benefited you in any number of ways. If you get an urge while balancing your checkbook, think about the financial hardships you've endured due to your addictions, if that was the case for you. Every time you get an urge to indulge, recall the specific harm your addictive behavior caused.

Everything you do from this moment on will be centered on remaining vice-free. Whether you're getting up in the morning, working during the day, or going to sleep at night, your unwavering commitment will be to become and remain vice-free. Remind yourself that indulging in the vice means the death of everything you care about and what matters most. Indulging in this vice, indulging in any vice, would mean kissing it all goodbye. You can't let that happen. You won't let it happen.

Today and for every other day for as long as you live, you'll stubbornly refuse to be controlled by vices. From this day forward, you'll stand up and fight. Fight every temptation that rears its ugly head. Fight, dear reader, and don't stop fighting until you've conquered addiction, the enemy of your success and happiness.

If step 5 trained you for a fight, step 7 means stepping into the ring with your opponent, the vice in question. Step 7 is where you encounter temptation in the form of triggers, urges, and cravings. You'll also work with prelapses. Triggers, as you'll recall, are the external and internal cues that bring on urges and cravings. A prelapse is when you act on an urge or craving by taking a step toward the vice. For example, if your vice is watching internet porn, looking at the cover of the *Sports Illustrated* swimsuit issue counts as a prelapse.

When you catch yourself approaching or engaging in prelapse behavior, your job is to stop, admit that you've stepped over the line, and course correct. Immediately! Although the swimsuit issue isn't considered pornography, it's a slippery slope for porn addicts that will lead them back to hard-core porn. You know it will, so don't go there. But if it sneaks up on you and you suddenly notice you're in Barnes and Noble looking at sexy magazine covers, cease and desist. Leave the magazine section immediately, and head over to the self-help section, where you'll find plenty of recovery books you can check out instead.

A prelapse can be solely internal as well. For example, if you catch yourself fantasizing about sex while driving home from work, and you don't stop once you catch yourself, that counts as a prelapse. Or, if you're recovering from alcoholism, you might catch yourself reminiscing about the good old days and what it was like to hang out at your favorite pub. You catch yourself romanticizing and glorifying your drinking. This could happen while you're eating breakfast, running, or commuting to work.

Though it's only in your imagination, it still counts as a prelapse if it's something you engage in for an extended period. In other words, it's not just a passing thought that triggers you briefly but doesn't last. When the initial thought begins as a trigger and you run with it, it's advanced to the status of a prelapse. If you fail to recognize it as a prelapse, fail to stop it and move on, you're headed for a lapse and then a relapse. Learning to identify and neutralize triggers and prelapses, both external and internal, along with the urges and cravings that come with them, is the role of step 7.

What if you're unable to resist temptation? What if you try but can't neutralize it? What then? First, make sure you have tried everything—twice. If you find you're still unable or unwilling to say no to a craving, if a prelapse turns into a lapse and the lapse turns into a relapse, so be it. That's right. Go right ahead and relapse, but be strategic about it. Be deliberate. Consider it fieldwork. You're gathering information that will shed light on the true nature of your addictive behavior. You're doing research that requires indulging in the vice. However, and this is a big *however*, pay close attention to what happens and how you feel before, during, and after you indulge.

Start by asking yourself one or more of the following questions:

Prelapse Questions

1. Will it really be all I imagine and hope it will be? Why or why not?
2. When it's over, will I be satisfied or feel cheated, as if I didn't quite get my money's worth? Why or why not?
3. Will I feel good about having done it? Why or why not?
4. Will I feel good about myself? Why or why not?
5. Is there something I'll wish I had done instead? Is there some better way I could have spent my time? What would that be?
6. If I could get myself to do the alternative activity instead of indulging in the vice, would I? Why or why not?
7. Will the benefits of indulging outweigh the drawbacks, or will the drawbacks outweigh the benefits? Explain.
8. What are some likely long-term drawbacks of indulging? Explain. (See "Addiction Buster 3.")
9. What are some of the long-term benefits of abstaining? Explain.
10. Simply put, will indulging be worth it? Why or why not?

We both know that the answer to that last question is it won't be worth it. It never is.

Still, you may have to repeat the experiment. Your rational mind understands that indulging is a bad idea, but your emotional mind thinks otherwise, and in the heat of the moment, your emotional mind wins out. These two mental subsystems are at odds, and emotions typically get the upper hand. Remember, feelings run the show. This research project may have to continue for a while, maybe even a long while. The vice won't go down without a fight. But instead of simply surrendering to the addiction, you'll plan ways to put it out of commission. You'll observe how your addiction operates, all the while strategizing ways to overthrow it. Yes, it has the upper hand for now but not forever—and maybe, if you work diligently, not for long.

Part of you desperately wants to be free of this vice that's keeping you down, preventing you from realizing your potential. But until you make the shift and can see through the vice, seeing it for what it is, cravings are inevitable, and relapses are likely.

It's all but inevitable that you'll periodically lose your footing, unable to resist temptation. You can't prevent cravings from arising just because you want to. Neither can you stop yourself from relapsing merely by insisting that you do. You can't make yourself do or not do something just because you'd prefer it. It takes more than that. It takes more than a preference backed by willpower to eliminate cravings and abolish addictive behaviors. Wanting it isn't enough. Willing it won't make it so.

Start by acknowledging the reality of the situation, and you stand a better chance of winning the war, though not every battle. At least for now, cravings are beyond your control, and therefore cannot rightfully be judged as good or bad. Once a craving has grabbed hold of you, or you've relapsed, you've lost control of that behavior. That's why you're no longer in a position to judge it. A craving or a relapse is best viewed as irrelevant. That's right. The fact that you relapsed is irrelevant.

But where does that leave you in your quest to become vice-free? If you can't control your cravings or stop yourself from relapsing, and if you view your cravings and relapses as irrelevant, what chance do you have of putting a stop to your addictive behavior? How are you to become vice-free? The answer is—drumroll, please—training!

It's not the craving or the relapse you have control over. It's your response that's within your control. Control how you react to them, and see what happens to the craving and relapse. If you're experiencing a craving, decide how best to respond. What *Breakaway Recovery* strategy or tool can you apply to the craving? That's where you want to place your attention—not on the craving itself but how you plan to counter it. Can you see the distinction and why it's important to focus only on your response?

If you've relapsed, keep your attention off the relapse, and concentrate on your response. Ask yourself, "What's next? What do I do now that I've relapsed?" And start with this: Never, I repeat, never respond with remorse, self-contempt, self-recrimination, or any other negative reaction. There's nothing to feel bad about. Addiction is not only part of the human condition—it *is* the human condition, and thus it's unavoidable. Everyone is addicted to something or many things. Getting beyond it is a process every serious quitter must deal with, and relapse is a part of that process.

You can't just choose not to drink to excess, not to binge watch the latest, greatest Netflix series, or not to eat a pint of ice cream. You first have to learn how to say no to your urges and cravings and live contentedly without your vices. It's a process, and choosing to engage in that process is only the first step. Don't expect this to be easy or quick. Don't expect it to go off without a hitch. Becoming and remaining vice-free takes work. Fortunately for you, it's work that comes with payoffs that can be astronomical.

To get those payoffs, you'll have to follow step 7 to the letter. Pay special attention to the word "any," as in, "If at any time you feel tempted to resume the addictive behavior ..." The first half of step 7 tells us we can't afford to let any trigger, temptation, urge, or craving go unrecognized. Once recognized, you must address it and counter the temptation using one or more of the *Breakaway Recovery* strategies. This book shows you how to do just that by introducing you to the *Breakaway Recovery* addiction busters, reframe journaling, the real-time technique, early rapid reinterpretation, and more. You'll build an arsenal of weapons that will make you invincible when it comes to fending off temptation. Yes, invincible! You'll have the vices shaking in their boots.

And let's not forget that while relapses, strategic or not, may sometimes be unavoidable, it makes sense to avoid relapsing whenever possible. You can do this, in part, by avoiding toxic environments. Avoiding toxic environments means staying out of bars, nightclubs, porn sites, casinos, and the like. However, it doesn't mean entirely steering clear of your triggers. Don't go out of your way to avoid driving by a nightclub or a strip joint, for example. Just don't stop and go inside. You don't want to restrict your life, fearing that you'll give in to temptation whenever a trigger shows up. Triggers will show up. They're everywhere. You couldn't avoid them all even if you tried. Deliberately visiting porn sites or hanging out in bars for no good reason is another matter. If you have a good reason to be in a bar, attending a friend's birthday party, for example, it's okay.

You want to be able to confront your triggers, not run away from them. Ultimately, you want to neutralize them. Your goal is to dismantle your triggers, removing their power over you. This isn't about resisting cravings for the rest of your life. It's about eliminating them, once and for all. You'll get so that you don't want to smoke the cigarette, eat the ice cream, or drink the whiskey. There will be no temptations to resist, no cravings to battle. When that time comes, you still want to avoid toxic environments, but it will be easier to do that. Hanging around drunks at a bar will no longer be attractive. Instead, you'll see it as an intellectual and spiritual wasteland. You have nothing to gain by hanging out in such an environment.

The rule is this: avoid toxic environments whenever possible, and confidently confront your triggers when they're unavoidable.

You may find that taking step 6 isn't as easy as you thought or hoped it would be, and despite your best efforts, you're not able to respond skillfully to triggers, temptations, prelapses, lapses, or relapses. You may find yourself being carried out of the ring on a stretcher on the first day you take step 6 with a particular vice. That's not a problem. It simply means you're not ready to take on the vice in question. What would you do if you were about to get into a boxing ring with Mike Tyson? If you didn't know much about boxing or even who Mike Tyson was, you'd check out his training videos on YouTube. You'd learn about the way he trained for a fight and fought opponents. It's all about preparation. If you're up against an especially potent vice, you have to rethink your training routine.

When you can't resist indulging, when you get knocked out in the ring (i.e., you relapse), it always means the same thing: You have a skills deficit brought on by a training deficit. More training is required. That last bit is the good news. You may not be able to resist temptation, but you can discipline yourself to train harder and smarter. With enough of the right kind of training, you'll acquire the skills needed to knock out your opponents, all of them, in good time.

If you've already read through the book once, now you're ready to do the work and take the steps. Step 7 is a good time to put the addiction busters to work, using them in conjunction with the prelapse questions. The addiction busters will help you answer the prelapse questions, giving you the best chance of warding off the temptation. If this is your first time through, keep reading. Once you've read the entire book, start from the beginning and follow the instructions, taking each step in turn until you have eliminated the addiction. Then start again with the next vice on your list and continue in this way until you have eliminated all of your addictive behaviors. Can you do it? You can if you think you can and if you do the work and follow the instructions.

Step 8

If for any reason, you break your commitment to abstaining from the addictive behavior, set another quit date and resume the above steps until you have permanently eliminated it from your list.

So, you relapsed. Surprised? You needn't be. Relapsing, like it or not, is a part of the process. Maybe you know that from reading this book. Maybe you had no idea. But once you've decided to drop a bad habit, eliminate a vice, or break out of an addictive rut, you may have to relapse one or more times before your decision to quit sticks. Each of us will experience a certain number of relapses before achieving abstinence. None of us knows what that number is, but when you relapse, you've moved one step closer to hitting that final number.

This movement toward sustained abstinence is called a prolapse because every relapse is an opportunity to go back through the steps and see what you missed the last time around. It's an opportunity to strengthen your mindset and to sharpen your skill set. There's nothing wrong with that. Step 8 is where you'll turn a relapse into a prolapse. It's an extension of the fieldwork you started in step 7. It's where you discover what's missing and what's needed to do away with the vice once and for all.

You may automatically assume that relapsing is a setback or, worse yet, an outright failure for which you can't help but feel discouraged. Well, I'm here to tell you it's not. There are no failures. Think of it as a chance to learn what works and what doesn't. Relapsing, as we learned in step 7, is a positive (pro) not a negative (con) event. While a relapse or even a minor lapse is typically thought of as a problem, think of a prolapse as an opportunity, and so the bigger the relapse, the bigger the opportunity.

The stronger your opponent, the stronger the response you need to generate. The stronger the response you generate, the stronger you become as a recovery warrior, and it starts with refusing to feel discouraged. How? By realizing you have no reason to feel discouraged and that feeling discouraged will only make matters worse. Instead, feel inspired to fight on, knowing that it's only a matter of time before you win the war. If you continue to train, if you continue to fight, you're bound to come out on top. Let the relapse inspire you to double your efforts. Then double them again!

You may think, "But if I welcome the inevitable relapses and see them as learning opportunities on the path to recovery, I'll use that thinking as an excuse to relapse." Maybe so. But if you want to relapse, you'll use any reason available. You won't even need a reason. You'll simply give in to temptation. And while relapsing may be part of the process, it doesn't have to be the biggest part. You don't have to keep relapsing. You don't even have to relapse one more time. It's one option, but it's not the only option. You can learn from your previous relapses.

It's true that you can deliberately indulge in the vice as a learning experience that will open your eyes to the futility of maintaining the addictive behavior. This is a viable strategy for overcoming your addictive behavior. It's also true that you can use this strategy to deceive yourself, using it as an excuse to indulge. While this is one of many possible strategies, it comes with risks and consequences. Use it as a last resort and only after you've exhausted all your other options. But if those other options have failed, don't rule out relapsing intentionally as a learning experience.

For example, you can try smoking a whole pack of cigarettes, one cigarette after another, without stopping, until you've smoked the whole pack. Notice how that makes you feel about smoking. Do that, and I guarantee it will be a while before you light up another cigarette. Beware, however! Smoking a whole pack of cigarettes could hasten your path toward lung cancer or give you a heart attack. Of course, any way you smoke cigarettes can do that, but this exercise will speed up the process.

If you'd rather not do that, and I suggest you don't, try cutting down your indulgence by 75% to see how that feels. For example, watch 75% less TV, and be sure not to use a substitute like YouTube. No substituting screen time of any sort or any other vice. Substitute only sanctioned, healthy activities. Meditate, call or visit a friend, go for a walk, or read a good book. Then you can watch 25% of the TV time you've allotted. With these attempts at moderation, you may find you end up going over the time limit, watching more TV than you committed to. Abstinence, it turns out, is easier than moderation. There may be no getting around it. You have to give up certain vices altogether, at once. The rule will be no TV, not less TV, or no cigarettes, not fewer cigarettes.

If you do decide to relapse, you want to be sure you do it for the right reason, using it to gain insight into the futility of indulging in the vice. You're reluctantly but deliberately relapsing now so you won't have to relapse later. You can only do this if you remain mindful of what happens during and after your relapse.

When the relapse is over, ask yourself one or more of the 10 relapse questions that come next. Notice that these questions are virtually the same as the prelapse questions, but they are to be used after a relapse instead of before a relapse. Answering these questions honestly will help turn the relapse into a prolapse, making it less likely that you'll relapse again. Make sure you write or type your answers in your reframe journal (presented in the next chapter) so you can review them later. Writing, reviewing, and updating your answers is essential to the process. For sample answers, see the end of this section.

Relapse Questions

1. Was indulging in the vice really all I expected or hoped it would be? Why or why not?
2. Now that it's over, do I feel satisfied, or do I feel cheated, as if I didn't quite get my money's worth? Why or why not?
3. Am I pleased with having done it, or do I regret it? Why or why not?
4. Do I feel good about it? Why or why not?
5. Do I feel good about myself? Why or why not?
6. Is there something I wish I had done instead, a better way I could have spent my time? What could that have been?
7. If I could go back in time and do the alternative activity instead of indulging in the vice, would I? Why or why not?
8. Did the benefits outweigh the drawbacks, or did the drawbacks outweigh the benefits? Explain.
9. What are some likely long-term drawbacks of indulging and some of the long-term benefits of abstaining? Explain.
10. Simply put, was it worth it? Why or why not?

All vice is detrimental, but when you're dealing with a supernormal stimulus, indulging means you're depleting your brain's happy chemicals both in the short and long term. If you're watching porn more days than not, anywhere from 30 minutes to five hours at a time, this puts a considerable strain on your hormonal and neurotransmitter systems. You deplete your dopamine, oxytocin, serotonin, endorphin, and other mood-regulating neurotransmitters.

As we've seen, dopamine is the chemical involved in motivating you to pursue goals. When you watch porn, clicking around from one video to the next, you use up your available store of dopamine, leaving nothing left for your other projects and tasks. Your other projects and tasks also begin to pale in comparison to the supernormal stimuli of those pornographic images. Your brain's reward system is compromised.

At no time in our history have we had access to anything close to the modern pornographic images that trick our brains into thinking we are having sex with multiple partners both consecutively and simultaneously. We've never experienced anything close to what we experience when watching porn. And no, our brains can't tell the difference between sex with the images on the screen and a real person. Young kids growing up with porn prefer screen sex over sex with a real, live person. Our brains evolved to pursue novelty, and porn certainly gives us that. Unfortunately, there's something called too much of a "good" thing.

Here's what you can expect when you get too much of the good thing called porn or any other supernormal stimulus: Your dopamine store runs out. This means you have less motivation and less interest in pursuing the things that really matter to you. Watching porn (or gambling or gaming or shopping or overeating or any other vice) becomes your priority, and you neglect your other interests. Your attraction to images on the screen also devolves, getting more novel and kinkier or more and more perverted as time goes by. You develop fetishes that previously made your skin crawl.

Your brain's reward center, along with its motivation center, likewise becomes compromised, and the things that once brought you pleasure will no longer deliver. You find life to be dull and wake up feeling lost, lonely, and empty. The only way to escape these feelings involves turning to the screen. Only when you do, you need more porn to get the relief you crave. You also need more intense forms of porn to get the same relief. Unhappiness and lack of enjoyment and fulfillment are what you can expect if you insist on indulging in pornography or any other supernormal stimulus.

You simply can't be happy if you're addicted to a supernormal stimulus. It's unnatural. It's unsustainable. Being happy, fulfilled, and loving life requires you to live in agreement with reality. Having your face stuck to a screen streaming pornographic images isn't living in agreement with reality. It's living in agreement with a fantasy—and a pathetic one at that.

If you have depleted dopamine, you lose your drive and motivation for other activities. You lose interest in important projects and tasks, finding them boring because they can't compete with the supernormal stimulus. Your brain's pleasure center cannot reward you for important tasks because the vice depletes your happy chemicals, along with your motivation chemicals. Eventually nothing other than your drug of choice gives you the boost you crave, and soon even that won't help. You find yourself feeling lethargic and disinterested in life.

Now's a good time to take another look at the stages of change introduced in step 4. This is no time for bravado. If you're not ready, you're not ready. Identifying your stage of change determines what you should be working on in the 10 steps of *Breakaway Recovery*.

The Stages of Change

- Precontemplation
- Contemplation
- Determination
- Preparation
- Action
- Maintenance
- Conclusion or relapse

In the precontemplation stage, you don't know you have a problem. You haven't even thought about it. In the contemplation stage, you at least wonder if you have a problem. In the determination stage, you decide to do something about it. In the preparation stage, you get yourself ready to tackle the problematic behavior. You formulate a plan for addressing the problem.

In the action stage, you carry out your plan and take steps to address it. In the maintenance stage, you do whatever you feel is necessary to remain free of the problematic behavior. In the conclusion stage, the problem is behind you. You no longer care to indulge, so you no longer need to do anything related to the vice in question. It's simply no longer a threat or temptation. You can move on to bigger and better things.

Because you've gotten this far in the book, I assume you've already concluded that you have a problem and that you've decided you want to quit. Now you must decide that you will quit and will do whatever it takes to eliminate the vice in question. That's step 3 of *Breakaway Recovery* and the stages of change. If you haven't acknowledged that you've been indulging in a series of addictive behaviors (step 1), made a list of your addictive behaviors and arranged them in the order you plan to renounce them (step 2), resolved to abandon the entire range of your addictive behaviors (step 3), set a quit date to abandon and replace the vice in question (step 4), mobilized yourself for success (step 5), stopped indulging in the vice (step 6), or used one or more of the *Breakaway Recovery* addiction busters to counter temptations (step 7), go back and do that now. You may have assumed you could skip one or more of the steps—that you could half-ass your recovery. You can't. There are no shortcuts.

If you need step 8, that means you've relapsed. If you haven't relapsed and you're ready to take on the next vice on your list, you can move on to step 9. If you relapsed yesterday but haven't indulged today, you can set today as your new quit date for that vice. If you have indulged today, you can set tomorrow as your quit date. If, on the other hand, you relapsed and know damn well you're nowhere near being ready to quit the vice, you can push the date out to a month or longer, moving back to step 5 to get yourself ready before setting another quit date. This is how it works. It's a process with good days and bad days, ups and downs, and successes and failures. None of that is wrong or bad or worth fretting about. It's just the way breaking an addiction works.

Review the stages of change. Decide where you stand. Then move to the *Breakaway Recovery* step that's most appropriate for your stage of change. For example, if you're in the preparation stage with a particular vice, go back to *Breakaway Recovery* step 5, and take it from there.

When all is said and done, here's what you need to know about relapsing: It's about to happen. It's happening. It already happened. In all three cases, the relapse itself is irrelevant. Now, you might argue that in the case where it's about to happen, you can do something to stop it from happening. If that's the case, it's not about to happen. If it's about to happen, you're not doing anything to stop it. If it's happening, it's happening. If it already happened, it already happened. Again, in each case, the relapse itself is irrelevant. What matters is your response to the prelapse or the relapse.

You can respond skillfully or unskillfully. Responding unskillfully includes blaming yourself, someone else, or external circumstances. It means feeling defeated. You might catch yourself saying things like "I can't believe I relapsed again. I'll never get sober. I'm such a loser." None of this will help.

Here's what you can do instead: Start by accepting that you relapsed, then go beyond acceptance by turning the relapse to your advantage. Welcome it. Embrace it. Exploit it for all it's worth. View the relapse as nothing less than a perfect opportunity to apply the strategies, tactics, tools, and techniques detailed in this book, including answering the relapse questions introduced earlier. Respond in this way, and the relapse becomes one of the best things that could have happened.

This also applies to urges and cravings as well as to relapses that have already happened, to relapses about to happen, and to relapses in progress. Believe it or not, you can't always stop yourself from indulging, no matter how much you want to. You're not in charge of the universe. You're not even in charge of your own minuscule slice of it.

Even your own thoughts, emotions, desires, and behaviors often aren't yours to control.

When even despite your best efforts, you're still unable to control your behavior, accept it. Accept it as being exactly the way it should be, and turn the relapse to your advantage. Get it? It happened. Nothing can change that now. That's why it's irrelevant. What's relevant is how you respond to what happens, even when what happened is a relapse.

Don't get me wrong, I'm not suggesting you be cavalier about the relapse or brush it off as if it never happened. Just be sure that what you do about it doesn't make matters worse. Respond in a way that gives you the best chance of avoiding future relapses. And hey, if beating yourself up about it does the trick, by all means, beat yourself up. But that probably won't work. Use the tools detailed throughout this book to give you the best chance of succeeding. When you relapse, go back to step 4, and take it from there.

Then when you get to step 5, take your time enumerating the likely drawbacks that come with indulging. Look to the examples given in addiction buster 3. How is the addiction sabotaging your success and happiness?

Your vices clearly aren't worth the price you're paying.

Step 9

Continue to renounce each item on your list using the steps outlined above until you have eliminated the entire range of your addictive behaviors.

We've chosen a lofty goal. We've committed to eliminating all of our addictions and bad habits, past, present, and future. That's why it's essential to approach this as a lifelong process. You start by eliminating your most destructive addictions, things like drugs and alcohol, the ones that can kill you. Next, you tackle the vices that probably won't kill you but will kill your potential and your chances for success and happiness.

Once you've abandoned your addictions and your vices, you can start chipping away at your bad habits. This can be anything from biting your fingernails to interrupting the people you talk with. When you break a bad habit, you want to replace it with a good one, just as you replace your addictions and vices with empowering alternatives. For example, instead of complaining, express your gratitude. Instead of arguing, initiate conversations. Instead of preaching, try listening, and when you do talk, stop telling others what they should or shouldn't do. And instead of trying to win people over to your cause, try supporting someone else's cause for a change or support the rights of others to disagree with you.

Or, if you have a habit of interrupting people, practice active listening and allow them to complete their thoughts before chiming in, especially if you disagree with them. If you're like most of us, you're quick to form opinions and are willing to defend them with your life. (By the way, it's really your ego you're defending.) Really listen with an open mind to what others have to say and be willing to change your mind when appropriate. Make communicating in these ways your new habit.

Your outlook is also a habit. For example, you can be pessimistic and cynical or optimistic and affirmative. Stop insisting that something is not possible and start insisting that it can be done or at least is worth giving it a try. Whenever you catch yourself being a downer, pull yourself up. Find something, anything, to move you closer to your goal. Look for the good around you and in yourself and other people. It's there if you take the time to find it. Make this an empowering alternative habit, one that you use to replace your current negative habit of seeing only what's wrong with you, others, and the world.

Likewise, if you're in the habit of staying up late, start going to bed early. If you hit the snooze in the morning, put your alarm clock across the room and get out of bed and stay out of bed when it goes off. If you're in the habit of letting the dishes pile up in the sink, get in the habit of washing them as soon as you're finished using them. If you're in the habit of procrastinating, of putting off unpleasant tasks for later, develop the habit of doing unpleasant tasks first and getting them out of the way. Pay your bills as soon as they come in. Brush your teeth as soon as you're done eating. Fill up your gas tank once it goes below half a tank. Develop the habit of doing the things you don't want to do, the things you don't like to do, and the things you may not even know how to do (details on habit stacking coming up). Be the person who automatically does whatever it is that needs to be done. Then reward yourself with a pleasant task.

Breakaway Recovery isn't like the other recovery approaches you may have tried. It's not merely about getting sober or getting off drugs. It's a life-long process of gaining insights and achieving breakthroughs, transformation, and self-actualization. We measure our success by the degree to which we have mastered our habits, choosing this as the single aim of everything we think, feel, say, and do. How freaking cool is that?

Step 10

Share the message of vice-free living by helping others identify and eliminate their own addictive behaviors.

A time-tested strategy for learning any new skill or skill set is to teach it to others. To accelerate your own progress, find others you can teach. You can work together with one other person, or you can start a *Breakaway Recovery* group similar to an AA 12-step group. The idea is to learn the *Breakaway Recovery* skill set by sharing instructions and feedback about the progress made by each group member. Read this book together and talk about what's working, what isn't working, and why. Teach each other. Coach each other. Encourage each other. Set it up as a training academy versus a traditional support group, and use this book and its strategies as your curriculum. You'll find that as you teach newcomers, you're challenged to think deeply about how to best answer their questions and practice and apply the *Breakaway Recovery* skill set yourself.

You're reading this book because you want to eliminate your addictive behaviors. Despite the many obstacles you'll encounter along the way, the real obstacle is a skills deficit brought on by a training deficit. You've come to understand that addiction is a learned behavior and a choice among options, not a medical condition or chronic relapsing brain disease. Addiction is something you do, not something you have, and certainly not something you are. That's why you have to unlearn those learned behaviors and teach yourself to do something better and worthwhile.

Here's how:

Practice the 10 steps we introduced earlier as if your life depends on it. It does. To master all 10 steps, you have to engage in the optimal level of instruction, practice, coaching, and application of the *Breakaway Recovery* strategies, tools, and techniques, including and especially the *Breakaway Recovery* addiction busters and reframing skills. Not only will that bring you to the goal of being vice-free, but it will also open the door to previously unrecognized opportunities, unrealized potential, and yes, unimagined possibilities.

The *Breakaway Recovery* Addiction Busters

The addiction busters detailed in this section will help you understand and combat your addictive triggers, urges, and cravings. As you read through them, think about how they can assist you in taking the 10 steps. Each addiction buster gives you an effective strategy or technique for avoiding, neutralizing, or overcoming the various temptations you face. Each can also be used as a topic of discussion for *Breakaway Recovery* meetings you attend. Group members can share how they used an addiction buster to avoid or overcome a temptation.

Some of my clients find it helpful to pick a single buster and spend some time each day for a week thinking about it. They choose one they find particularly meaningful, and they consider how it applies to the vice they're working on. You'll find it helpful to keep the vice you're dealing with in mind as you read and contemplate one buster at a time.

These are the *Breakaway Recovery* addiction busters:

ADDICTION BUSTER 1

Acknowledge that your addiction is a learned behavior and a choice among options, not a medical condition. Take responsibility for your addictive behavior and decide, once and for all, that you will do whatever it takes to eliminate it.

Your recovery starts by acknowledging that your addictions are learned behaviors you choose to perform. You could stop, but you don't. It's not that you're not addicted to these behaviors. You are. But there's a big difference between addictive behaviors and medical conditions. Addictions are disorders, to be sure, but they're psychological disorders, not medical disorders. And as we've seen, your addictive behavior is driven in part by biological factors and the power of deeply ingrained habits. You're up against some powerful forces, yet that still doesn't mean addiction is a medical condition or that you can't resist those forces. It's not, and you can—not that stopping will be easy. Most likely, it won't. It'll be challenging.

Addiction buster 1 asks you to take on that challenge by accepting responsibility for your addictive behaviors and by deciding to do whatever it takes to eliminate those behaviors. This book shows you what it takes to do just that, starting with making that life-changing decision. If you haven't done it already, do it now. Decide, once and for all, to do whatever it takes to eliminate your addictive behaviors. (See step 3 of the 10 steps of *Breakaway Recovery*.)

This is addiction buster 1. Read it. Study it. Apply it. Master it.

ADDICTION BUSTER 2

In line with what's become known as Hebb's law (neurons that fire together wire together), each time you indulge in the addictive behavior, you wire your brain for more of the same. Indulging strengthens the hold an addictive behavior has on you by reinforcing the neural connections that make up its biological component. Conversely, each time you successfully refrain from indulging, those neural connections begin to weaken. With enough practice, you'll be free from the hold the addiction once had on you.

By indulging in addictive behavior, you're digging your own grave. The more ice cream you eat, the more cigarettes you smoke, the more beer you drink, the further down the hole of addiction you descend, and the harder it becomes to climb out. Fortunately, the longer you go without a cigarette, the better your chances of continuing to go without. Addiction buster 2 focuses on the importance of learning. We learn by doing and by practicing. Each time you smoke a cigarette, you're teaching yourself to smoke and you're practicing the act of smoking. You're also training yourself to light up every chance you get.

Alternatively, each time you deliberately refrain from lighting up, you're practicing the opposite: You're training yourself to be a nonsmoker, and you're wiring your brain to see yourself in a new, healthy light. It's not easy. It takes practice and chutzpah, but all worthwhile things do. And so it is with those behaviors that are not worthwhile. Learning to be an alcoholic, a crackhead, or a dope fiend likewise takes practice and chutzpah. You taught yourself to be addicted. You can empower yourself to be free.

That's right. You become addicted to your vices through practice. You had plenty of help from those who had a vested interest in your becoming addicted. This might include friends, family members, marketers, advertisers, salespersons, drug dealers, liquor store owners, and so on. These people may have helped teach you the steps to becoming addicted, and you acted as an all-too-willing victim. But there's good news. The way you became addicted is the same way you'll abandon your addictions, while replacing them with empowering alternatives.

The process, which I call the learning chain, works like this:

- Instruction
- Practice
- Coaching
- Application
- Mastery

The learning chain is the way we learn to do the things we do. It happens formally or informally. Someone shows us how to perform a certain behavior by giving us explicit instructions, telling us what to do, how to do it, when to do it, where to do it, and so on. Or we learn by watching others perform the behavior. For example, we watch our parents smoking. When they're not looking, we steal a couple of their cigarettes.

We get together with our friends, and we light up and smoke away. We may get sick the first few times, but that doesn't stop us from smoking again. We encourage each other to keep at it. Cool kids smoke, and we want to be one of the cool kids. Maybe the older kids we look up to show us how to inhale. We go off and practice and come back for more instruction and more coaching. In time, we've become experts at the art of smoking, and now we're one of the cool kids.

Whatever your vice may be, one way or another, you learned to indulge. Maybe you're an autodidact, a self-taught smoker, drinker, or gamer. As you made your way through the steps of the learning chain, you were rewarded with good feelings of one kind or another, and so you kept at it. Knowing this will help you overcome your addictive behavior, whatever it may be. You learned it. You can unlearn it and learn something else to take its place.

This is addiction buster 2. Read it. Study it. Apply it. Master it.

ADDICTION BUSTER 3

Prove to yourself that your addiction has hijacked your life—eroding your confidence, diminishing your potential, sabotaging your success, killing your dreams, and destroying your happiness. If you continue to indulge in this addictive behavior, you'll continue to experience the self-limiting consequences of everything from career failures and financial hardships to lost relationships and emotional turmoil. Frequently take time to contemplate the many painful consequences of indulging in the addictive behavior.

Just reading this buster, or any buster for that matter, is unlikely to help. You have to identify how the addictive behavior eroded your confidence, diminished your potential, sabotaged your success, killed your dreams, and destroyed your happiness. You have to come up with real-life examples, focusing on missed opportunities, career failures, financial hardships, lost relationships, mental anguish, emotional turmoil, loss of self-respect, and loss of freedom. It's a lot to think about but worth the effort.

Come up with as many examples as you can, write them in your journal, and review them frequently, at least once a day if that's what it takes to get in touch with the suffering you experienced. Just thinking about the pain or terrible losses you experienced is unlikely to stop you from indulging in the vice. You need to remember but also relive those consequences, especially how you felt at the time.

Did you miss out on getting a formal education because you were watching TV when you should have been doing your homework? Are you a janitor who wanted to be a teacher or a teacher who wanted to be a writer? How does that feel?

The following exercises are designed to help you come up with specific examples for how your addictive behavior negatively affected your life and prevented you from becoming the best version of yourself. Identify the exercises that apply to you and then come up with examples from your own life. Finally, use those examples of addictive behavior's impact to fuel your recovery.

Exercise 1: Eroding Your Confidence

Perhaps you felt embarrassed when meeting new people because you quit school due to your drug use and ended up cleaning houses for a living. You may have dreaded being asked what you do for a living, so you avoided invitations to parties or even weddings. One of my former counseling clients called her friend at the last minute, saying she couldn't attend her wedding because she caught the flu. In reality, she was scared she couldn't hold her own in conversations with other wedding guests. Can you identify with this? How are your vices eroding your confidence?

Exercise 2: Diminishing Your Potential

Perhaps you think of yourself as ordinary, a nobody, or an underachiever. But maybe, just maybe, behind that wall of addiction and low self-esteem lurks a genius or mad scientist. There may be an Einstein inside of you, just waiting to burst forth and make the next great scientific discovery. But you ignore the voice that wants more for you. It'll be drowned out by your addiction until you wake up and see what it's doing to you. How are your vices diminishing your potential?

Exercise 3: Sabotaging Your Success

Perhaps you failed to go to high school or college, or you dropped out due to your drinking or drugging. Then you settled for low-paying jobs or menial labor. It wasn't that you didn't have the ability to do better. You simply settled for less because hanging out with your druggie friends was familiar and easier than doing all the work required to make it through to graduation. Worse still, maybe you thought college applications were too complicated when you had a hangover, which was every time you sat down to fill them out. How are your vices sabotaging your success?

Exercise 4: Killing Your Dreams

Maybe you always dreamed of traveling to foreign lands but never had the wherewithal to make it happen. You were so caught up in drinking or gambling or shopping that traveling remained a dream that you believed would never come true. And you were right. As long as you stay committed to your drug of choice, it never can. But it doesn't have to be this way. You still have options. You still have time to realize your dream and do the things you are meant to do. The realization of those possibilities starts with giving up your vices. How are your vices killing your dreams?

Exercise 5: Destroying Your Happiness

Do you find yourself feeling unhappy some or most of the time? Do you fail to take pleasure in the simple things in life? Have your vices taken up so much of your time that you have little or no time left for the things that make (or would make) you happy? This is what vice does. It destroys what little happiness may be left in your life and blocks whatever happiness is possible. How are your vices destroying your happiness?

Exercise 6: Career Failures

Maybe you made it through college and started on the path to a promising career. But for some strange reason, your social drinking started escalating along with your career. Before you knew what was happening, your drinking outpaced your promotions, and you found yourself out of a job. It's hard to build a successful career when you stay out late drinking and show up hungover and late to work hungover. How are your vices contributing to your professional failures?

Exercise 7: Financial Hardships

Do you find yourself living beyond your means? Are your credit cards maxed out? Do you have bills you can't pay? Have you failed to build a nest egg for your retirement? Is a new car or a college education for your children out of reach because of what you're spending on your bad habits? How are your vices causing you financial hardships?

Exercise 8: Lost Relationships

Have your friends or family members cut you off due to your drinking or drugging? Did your spouse file for divorce because you refused to cut down or stop? Are your vices getting in the way of club memberships, social gatherings, and business associations? How are your vices interfering with your relationships?

Exercise 9: Mental Anguish

As you've already learned in this book, our one true problem in life is suffering, and suffering is always an emotional affair. It's emotional pain that comes in various forms, from grief and anxiety to panic and depression. Not all suffering is the result of addiction, but for many of us much of it is. How are your vices contributing to your mental anguish?

Exercise 10: Emotional Turmoil

Do you find yourself caught up in a whirlpool of constantly shifting emotions? Are you enthusiastic one minute and lethargic the next? Are you often at a loss for words regarding how you feel? Addictive behavior can leave you feeling emotionally unstable and confused, as if you are surrounded by chaos. Fueled by addictive behavior, turbulent emotions get in the way of your goals and aspirations. How are your vices contributing to your emotional turmoil?

Exercise 11: Loss of Self-Respect

Are you disappointed with who you've become? Do you find yourself behaving in ways you find deplorable? Maybe you've lost all sense of dignity because you lack self-control when it comes to indulging in your vices. Or you feel ashamed because you're unable to control your behavior and resist even the vices that you find repugnant. Perhaps you have sadly begun to see yourself as a pathetic excuse for a human being. How are your vices contributing to your loss of self-respect?

Exercise 12: Loss of Freedom

Has your independence been threatened or limited because of your addictive behavior? Maybe you've lost your license because of a DUI. Maybe you have limited visitation rights with your children because of your drinking. Worse still, maybe they only get to see you when they visit you in jail. It might not be as bad as all that, but your autonomy may be limited in other ways due to your addictive behaviors. How are your vices contributing to your loss of freedom?

Once you've developed your own examples of the suffering that comes with addiction, use them to motivate yourself to eliminate those vices, not to beat yourself up. Redirect your attention to the possibilities and opportunities that lie ahead as you abandon your vices and replace them with empowering alternatives.

This addiction buster is aimed at helping you see the futility of indulging in your vices. But be careful not to overdo it. It should help you feel disgust for the vice, not for yourself. You're not the enemy. Your vices are. Get it? It's an important distinction that may seem obvious but can be easily overlooked.

This is addiction buster 3. Read it. Study it. Apply it. Master it.

ADDICTION BUSTER 4

Research your addiction at the library or online. Learn everything you can about the harmful consequences to yourself and others that result when you engage in your addictive behaviors.

For example, if you're addicted to internet porn, go to YouTube and watch "The Great Porn Experiment," a TEDxGlasgow video by former physiology teacher Gary Wilson, or listen to cognitive neuroscientist Dr. Trish Leigh on her *P*rn Brain Rewire* podcast. You can also go to www.fightthenewdrug.org and watch videos about human trafficking, sex slavery, and the negative effects working in the porn industry has on porn stars.

If you spend two hours a day watching porn, spend two hours a day watching or reading anti-porn material. Any time you get an urge to watch porn, watch an anti-porn video instead. Continue doing this until your desire to watch porn is extinguished for good. Apply this same strategy to your many other addictive behaviors.

When you investigate the effects of indulging in porn and other unnaturally pleasurable supernormal stimuli, here's some of what you'll learn:

Indulging in vices, especially those of the supernormal-stimulus type, damages your prefrontal cortex. This decreases your ability to regulate your executive functions, such as attention, volition, problem-solving, decision-making, planning, and execution. Indulging in a vice means having less control over how you think, behave, and feel. It ultimately makes you feel worse, not better.

Engaging with a supernormal stimulus depletes the happy chemicals secreted from your brain's reward center, making it more and more difficult for you to find joy in life's healthy pleasures. Over time, you are less likely to feel good about your life—and about yourself. The more you indulge, the less happy you are, the fewer positive emotions you experience, and the more negative emotions you encounter. Healthy emotions show up with less frequency, duration, and intensity. Toxic emotions show up with more frequency, duration, and intensity. Did you get that? It's huge! As you indulge, you'll feel worse more often, for longer periods of time, and with greater intensity. Once you know this, really know it in your heart of hearts, quitting is easy, inevitable, and automatic.

Indulging in a supernormal stimulus damages neural pathways that connect the prefrontal cortex to the brain's reward center. It becomes more and more difficult for these two brain centers to communicate, and thus more difficult for you to experience pleasure. Even as the brain's reward center pumps out happy chemicals, the place where conscious experience takes place isn't receiving the message, leaving you feeling flat at best and downright miserable at worst.

Over time, you indulge in your vice with increasing frequency, duration, and intensity. These are the celebrated three training factors that professional athletes and other expert performers use to master their craft. In your case, your vice uses these same factors to take control of you. Addiction busters, along with the other tools presented in this book, show you how to take back that control. This means studying, practicing, and applying the *Breakaway Recovery* skill set with increasing frequency, duration, and intensity.

I know this sounds like an awfully big commitment. But whatever it takes to break free from these potential-killing vices, it will be well worth any effort you expend. Trust me. Your efforts will be highly rewarded. But to claim those rewards, you have to find out as much as you can about your addictive behaviors and the destructive consequences that come with them. Only when you realize just how destructive and painful those consequences are (to you and others) will you be willing and able to put down your vices—once and for all!

And as you proceed on this journey, keep in mind that while the porn industry is one of the most despicable businesses, the rest—tobacco, gambling, alcohol—are not much better. These industries ruin lives by distracting people from what they are capable of doing and preventing them from becoming the superstars they could be. If you support these industries by watching porn, smoking cigarettes, drinking alcohol, buying scratch tickets, or hanging out on social media, you have virtually no chance of becoming that superstar. Regardless of how uncomfortable it may initially be, get in touch with the harmful consequences of indulging in these supernormal stimuli and make the commitment to eliminate them from your life.

This is addiction buster 4. Read it. Study it. Apply it. Master it.

ADDICTION BUSTER 5

When temptation strikes, replace your old habit of indulging with the new habit of not indulging. Instead of focusing on the act of indulging, focus on the act of not indulging. Think of not indulging as something you're doing, not something you're not doing. It's an active maneuver, not a passive one. While others busy themselves with indulging, you'll be busy *not* indulging—and loving yourself for it.

When I quit smoking many moons ago, I used to pause and watch whenever the person I was with lit up and smoked a cigarette. I watched closely as the person smoked, reminding myself that lung cancer was a likely outcome and feeling grateful that it wasn't me. I paid attention to the whole process from lighting up to putting out the cigarette, and I congratulated myself for not doing the same thing. I counted not smoking as a victory, and I made it a point to revel in my success.

Years later when I quit drinking, I did the same thing. For about the first year or so, I continued to go to clubs and bars and hang out with my drinking buddies. I watched them drink, and I watched them get drunk and make fools of themselves. I focused on the fact that I wasn't getting drunk and making a fool of myself. Not drinking became my favorite new pastime. I kept quite busy not drinking, and yes, I loved myself for doing it.

Remind yourself throughout the day that you're not indulging in the vice. Focus on the act of not indulging, even when there's no temptation to indulge. Tell yourself, "Look, I'm not indulging!" Congratulate yourself. "Good job!" Give yourself praise. Reward yourself. Appreciate the fact that you're not indulging. Enjoy it. Delight in it. Wallow in it. Bask in it. It's a big deal, a very big deal.

You don't even have to wait until temptation strikes to appreciate that you're not indulging. Any time you notice others are busy indulging and you're not, or any other time you notice you're not indulging, you can pause and appreciate that. Depending on your vice, say something to yourself, like "Cool, I'm not drinking. I'm not drunk. I'm not hung over."

This is addiction buster 5. Read it. Study it. Apply it. Master it.

ADDICTION BUSTER 6

Deliberately reject your desire to indulge in the addictive behavior. Redirect your attention away from your triggers or cravings to an activity that's important to you. Then keep doing what's important until the cravings subside. When the occasion for indulging passes, congratulate yourself and put another notch on your *Breakaway Recovery* belt. Take time to appreciate the fact that you're no longer ruled by the addictive behavior. Remind yourself of the advantages of not indulging and contemplate the benefits of being free from the addictive behavior.

If you're a low-bottom addict, if you've lost touch with what matters and your life revolves around your vices, then you need to look around for what you've abandoned. You need to discover what matters. It's there. Everyone has something or someone they care about or could care about. Maybe it's your spouse whom you've been ignoring. Maybe it's your health that you've been neglecting. Maybe it's a career that you've been spending less and less time pursuing. Find what that something is for you, and get busy devoting your time and energy to embracing it. When a craving strikes, shift your attention away from the vice, and focus on something or someone you know is so much more important than another artificial high.

Engross yourself in the alternative behavior, and soon enough, the craving to indulge in the vice will recede, leaving you with another notch on your *Breakaway Recovery* belt. What could be better than that? You're on your way, one step closer to vice-free living. Always take time to celebrate your victories, even if for just a few seconds. A quick pat on the back will go a long way to keeping you on track.

Even when you have no cravings or desire to indulge in the vice, and you are engaging in a positive behavior, congratulate yourself for not indulging and for no longer wanting to indulge. Think, "Hey, I'm not out drinking, and I have no desire to drink. How cool is that?"

This is addiction buster 6. Read it. Study it. Apply it. Master it.

ADDICTION BUSTER 7

Recall the one thing you want more than anything else, certainly more than you want to be addicted to this vice. This is the one thing that would make you happier than anything else, certainly much happier than the vice can ever make you. (If you don't know what that is, find out, then return and continue here.) Now, think about all the benefits and rewards associated with the one thing. Think about how it would improve your life—the way you feel about your life, the way you feel about yourself. Notice how the vice pales in comparison and acknowledge that the two are incompatible. To get your one thing, you have to renounce the vice, eliminating it from your life once and for all. Only then will you have room for your one thing. When the love of your one thing eclipses the love of your vice, your attraction to the vice will vanish into thin air, leaving you free to pursue and enjoy that which you want more than anything else.

If you struggle with one or more of the more serious addictions, such as heroin, cocaine, alcohol, or all the above, you are likely to be new to the idea of having a calling in life. You may not know what you want right now, never mind what the one thing you want more than anything else could possibly be. That's okay. You can start to give it some thought: "If I could have anything I wanted, do anything I wanted, or be anyone I wanted, what or who would that be?"

Although you may not know the answers to those questions, or you are afraid to ask them, go ahead and ask anyway. What seems impossible now will seem less unlikely as you start eliminating your vices. For now, you can skip this buster and come back to it later. This is true for all the busters. Find one or more that seem appropriate, practice those, and experiment. Everyone is different, so not every strategy or tool will be best for everyone who reads this book. Also, what works best for overcoming one vice may not work best for overcoming another. Still, addiction buster 7 is certainly a powerful approach. If you're not ready for this level of commitment, keep your eyes on it and be willing to come back to it in due time.

This is addiction buster 7. Read it. Study it. Apply it. Master it.

ADDICTION BUSTER 8

Be relentless and uncompromising when applying addiction buster strategies. Apply one or more of these techniques to every addictive trigger, thought, fantasy, feeling, and behavior you experience. Acknowledge and challenge them all. In this way, you can eliminate the entire range of your addictive behaviors.

If you aspire to be a serious quitter, the eighth buster is essential to your success when it comes to overcoming your addictive behaviors. As I've mentioned before, *Breakaway Recovery* is not for everyone—certainly not for the faint of heart. *Breakaway Recovery* is for serious quitters of addictive behaviors and for those aspiring to become serious quitters. If that's you, you'll have to be ruthless when it comes to dealing with your vices. Yes, you heard that right. Ruthless! You'll need to be relentless, tenacious, at times audacious, and perhaps occasionally ferocious. Think of Mike Tyson in his prime. When that's what it takes, you'd better be willing to be like Mike.

If all of this sounds like too much, know that there is an end in sight. Remember, the goal of *Breakaway Recovery* is to become vice-free by eliminating the entire range of our addictive behaviors. And while becoming vice-free may seem like a pipe dream for some of you, let me assure you it's not. It can be done, and I know because I've done it myself.

Go back and look at my vice list on page 85. You may be tempted to wonder, "Why would I want to give up all that pleasure? Hell, what's the point of that?" The point is you're going to replace those vices with something better—something much better or something much, much better. Don't be fooled by your addictions. Your vices have nothing of real value to offer you. If you want real happiness, real satisfaction, and real success, it starts with eliminating the very things that have held you back. And while the previous addiction busters tell you what to do, addiction buster 8 shows you how to do it.

This is addiction buster 8. Read it. Study it. Apply it. Master it.

You are now in possession of a powerful and effective recovery system. Dedicate yourself to working with *Breakaway Recovery*, and with the help of what's coming in the next two chapters, you'll find yourself inhabiting a whole new world that will both amaze and delight you. Read on.

6

RECOVERY IS A THOUGHT AWAY

Our life is shaped by our mind; we become what we think.
—Buddha

As I look back over my life, I realize I've been fortunate to have experienced many important milestones. Three stand out, as I begin this chapter. First was my introduction to martial arts, where I acquired a love of learning and deep respect for discipline. Then there was the day I decided to give up drinking. These two milestones opened the door to many opportunities I would otherwise never have enjoyed.

The third milestone, which in some ways could be considered the most important of all, was the day I discovered reframing. Reframing is perhaps the most fundamental and essential of the many psychological tools at our disposal. Take it to heart, and you'll see what I mean.

What Is Reframing?

Reframing is at the heart of not only what it takes to become and remain free from vices but also from the emotional torment that comes with addiction. Although I must admit, it's a bit misleading to say I'll introduce you to reframing since I've discussed it in one way or another throughout the previous sections of this book, along with examples of what reframing can do. Still, I haven't yet provided you with a formal definition or a detailed set of instructions for the actual practice of reframing, and it is the practice of reframing that brings the other *Breakaway Recovery* strategies to life.

Let's take a closer look at reframing—what it can do and how to do it.

The material we've covered up to this point could potentially get you sober. If so, great. But if you want to go beyond sobriety, if you have even higher aspirations and are intent on making the most of yourself and your life, you need to do the work that the less committed among us fail to do. This includes doing the tasks you don't want to do, don't like to do, or may not even know how to do. To be successful in life, you must never put off doing the things that need to be done, no matter how distasteful, tedious, or difficult those tasks may be. That's also true if you want to succeed in becoming and remaining vice-free. You must be willing to do things you won't always feel like doing. For our purposes, that starts with doing the tasks in this chapter—specifically, reading a set of instructions and then following those instructions.

If you've already managed to get sober, eliminated your major vices, or managed to eliminate all of them, learning to reframe might seem like overkill. You may, in fact, have eliminated your vices without doing the work of learning how to reframe. But if you want to go beyond sobriety, which is an impressive accomplishment in itself, then learning how to reframe is essential.

Although you're unlikely to find reading *any* set of instructions to be a fascinating experience, you will find the results of reading *these* instructions to be highly rewarding and, at the risk of sounding overly dramatic, life altering. You may initially find yourself resisting this assignment, but doing it will be worth every ounce of effort you expend. And once you get the hang of reframing, I can assure you it will be one of the most worthwhile things you have ever done, and you'll soon grow to love the practice. As one of my clients asked me, "Why haven't I heard about this before?! Why don't they teach this in schools?" Why, indeed?

Okay, let's say you're willing to accept that maybe, just maybe, learning how to reframe is, in fact, a worthwhile endeavor. But if reading and following instructions is one of your least favorite things to do, as it is for so many of us, you may have to force yourself to do it. I remember when I bought my stationary bike. It looked so beautiful in the display room. I hopped on and gave it a try. I loved it. I had to have it. I bought the bike and had it delivered to my house. To my dismay, it came in a box with the words "assembly required" and "instructions included." Even more dismaying, I was the one who had to read those instructions and assemble the bike. It was no easy task. I'll be honest, I saw it as a nightmare. The directions barely made sense, and they were pages and pages long. Still, after much trial and error, I managed to put it together, and once the ordeal was over, I could hardly have been happier.

I promise, the reframe instructions that follow will be much less daunting. If you're hesitant and would rather stick your head in a hot oven, then you'll just have to get behind yourself and push. That's right. Push yourself to read the instructions. Once you've done that, give yourself a pat on the back. Then start following them, and before you know it, you'll be reframing your way to a wiser, happier, more successful you.

Now you're about to learn not only what it takes to become and remain vice-free but also what it takes to become and remain happy—and happier than many would say you have a right to be.

Reframing, as you shall see, is at the heart of recovery from addiction. Everyone who has ever given up an addiction has done so by reframing, consciously or unconsciously. Whether we realize it or not, we overcome our vices by changing the way we think about them. Experience changes our perspectives, so we no longer find the vice attractive. In time, we come to find it repulsive. For example, that final horrendous hangover convinces us that drinking is not all it's cracked up to be. Our experience has reframed the way we view the vice. But formal reframing, reframing on purpose, can do even more than that. It's also at the heart of creating a life you love once you've gotten sober. And isn't that what it's all about, loving life?

Isn't it why we indulge in vices in the first place? Isn't it the reason we do everything we do? Surely it is.

But many, if not most of us, have given up on this lofty goal, and some have never even considered such a thing. "Loving life? Are you kidding? I'd be happy just to get through the day without having a nervous breakdown."

Well, I can assure you that you can learn to get through the day without having a nervous breakdown. And then you can go one better by getting through the day with a wide and heartfelt smile on your face. Reframing is the key to doing just that. And if you're one of the rare few who already love your life, be prepared to fall in love all over again, only this time deeper in love than ever.

So, what is reframing? Reframing is the practice of identifying, assessing, and reassessing life's seemingly unfavorable conditions until you view those conditions in the best light possible. It's the practice of changing the way we think and feel and how we act in response to our environment— the people, places, and events we encounter. It's the practice of turning whatever happens or doesn't happen to our advantage.

The following instructions will teach you how to make these positive changes in the way you experience your reality. Read and follow these instructions carefully, and you'll be on your way to loving the person you'll become and the life you'll create. Yes, reframing is that powerful.

As you've seen, the thing that gets in the way of becoming the person you want to be and accomplishing the things you want to accomplish is the psychological cage called addiction. That cage has been locked tight, keeping you from the things that would bring you reliable happiness and fulfillment, if only you could reach them. But you can't. That's the bad news. But as we've seen, there's also good news. We are capable of escaping from the cage of addiction, and I'm about to hand you the key that unlocks that cage.

Your bad habits, vices, and addictions, along with the painful emotions that come with them, are all the result of one primary cause—a set of self-defeating beliefs. And it's those beliefs we turn to now. With the help of reframing instructions and examples, you'll learn to identify the core beliefs that hold you back from living a life you love.[18]

With reframing, you learn how to put the lie to each and every one of those beliefs. When you do, the cage will swing open, and you'll be free to walk out. Free at long last! But there's more. Along with the beliefs that have kept you addicted to your vices, you have a host of additional beliefs that have kept you feeling angry, anxious, depressed, embarrassed, jealous, envious, nostalgic, sentimental, lonely, sad, and confused. These emotional torments, like your addictions, are also the result of your beliefs and the constant chatter in your mind. Here's where you learn to identify, challenge, and remove those core beliefs and the related thoughts they engender, replacing them with empowering alternatives.

Hang on to your seat. You're about to learn how to think straight and feel not merely good but great! Tony the Tiger great. Once you can do that, the world will be your oyster.

It's time to learn how to reframe your way not only to a life free from the ball and chain of addiction but also to a life of uncommon success and happiness. That's "Success" with a capital *S* and "Happiness" with a capital *H*.

Reframe Instructions and Examples

The reframing process begins with noticing that you don't like the way you're feeling. For example, you feel bored, angry, lonely, or in some other way unhappy. Once you notice the unpleasant emotion, record it in your journal and then look for the trigger. What do you feel bad about? Once you identify the trigger that sparked your emotional reaction, record the person, place, situation, or event that activated it. Then move on to identifying the self-defeating thought you had about the trigger.

The next step is to eliminate and replace that thought with a

---

18   Thank you, Albert Ellis, creator of rational emotive behavior therapy, the first and still the best of the cognitive behavior therapies.

self-empowering alternative. Then do the same with your self-defeating behaviors. Rehearse the self-empowering behavior. Identify your new feeling. Create a slogan to summarize how you'll carry out the self-empowering behavior, and later come back to your journal and record any observations about the situation after some time has passed.

Read through the simple step-by-step instructions and examples before attempting to do a reframe of your own. After you've read and understood them, come back and start with a two-step reframe, then a four-step reframe, then a six-step reframe, then an eight-step reframe, and finally a 10-step reframe. Once you've done that and feel you have the hang of reframing, you're on your way to becoming an expert reframer.

Keep this in mind once you've developed a daily reframe practice: You won't always have to do a full 10-step reframe. With a busy schedule, you may have limited time on your hands. When that's the case, you may decide to do a two-step reframe, using the self-defeating and the self-empowering thoughts. That gets to the heart of the matter. If you have a little more time, add the self-defeating and the self-empowering behavior steps. Do as many of the steps as time allows, with all 10 steps being the ideal.

Two-Step Reframe Instructions

Step 1

Feeling: Take out your reframe journal. On the first line, record your emotion or emotions.

Step 2

Trigger: On the second line, identify and record the conditions (i.e., circumstance, person, situation, or event) that triggered your emotional reaction. Be brief and objective when describing the trigger. Record only what actually happened, not your opinion about what happened. Stick to the facts.

Two-Step Reframe Example

Feeling: Excited.

Trigger: It's Friday night, and my old drinking buddies invited me out to a club to hear a blues band.

Practice the two-step reframe for a few days before moving on to the four-step reframe. The two-step reframe will help you get in touch with your emotions and the situations or events that trigger those emotions. After becoming familiar with your reactions and triggers, you can move on to the rest of the instructions below.

Four-Step Reframe Instructions

Step 1

Feeling: Take out your reframe journal. On the first line, record your emotion or emotions.

Step 2

Trigger: On the second line, identify and record the conditions (i.e., circumstance, person, situation, or event) that triggered your emotional reaction. Be brief and objective when describing the trigger. Record only what actually happened, not your opinion about what happened. Stick to the facts.

Step 3

Self-Defeating Thought: Now is the time to record your opinion about what happened. What is your story? What are you telling yourself about the trigger? It should be expressed in no more than one sentence. You may notice that you have more than one self-defeating thought about the trigger. But for now, stick to just one. Later, you'll learn how to handle the multiple self-defeating thoughts that come with most triggers.

Step 4

Self-Empowering Thought: Now, on the line immediately below the self-defeating thought, talk yourself out of your self-defeating belief. In doing this, you can use one or more strategies, including questions, logic, reasoning, arguments, evidence, facts, statistics, lists, examples, comparisons, and humor. You can also use stories, metaphors, slogans, quotes, and anything else you can think of to put the lie to your self-defeating thought. Finish off your argument with a powerful, one-sentence statement that counters the self-defeating thought.

Four-Step Reframe Example

Feeling: Excited.

Trigger: It's Friday night, and my old drinking buddies invited me out to a club to hear a blues band.

Self-Defeating Thought: It would be really fun to go out and have a couple of beers and listen to some tunes with my old buddies.

Self-Empowering Thought: It might start out as fun, but in the end, it would be a horror show. After the first drink, I'd feel extremely remorseful for having blown my sobriety. But I'd keep drinking anyway. As usual, I'd overdo it and make a fool of myself. Then I'd black out, get in a fight, smash up my car, or get arrested. How do I know? I know because that's what I've done every time I drank for the last three years. My drinking has progressed to a state where it's unquestionably out of control! How much more evidence do I need? *I can't drink safely!!!* The jig is up. It's over. If I decide to drink tonight, it will be to get wasted. There is no "only a couple of beers" for me—only another bender that will lead me to jail or worse. No thanks, I'm not interested.

Six-Step Reframe Instructions

Step 1

Feeling: Take out your reframe journal. On the first line, record your emotion or emotions.

Step 2

Trigger: On the second line, identify and record the conditions (i.e., circumstance, person, situation, or event) that triggered your emotional reaction. Be brief and objective when describing the trigger. Record only what actually happened, not your opinion about what happened. Stick to the facts.

Step 3

Self-Defeating Thought: Now is the time to record your opinion about what happened. What is your story? What are you telling yourself about the trigger? It should be expressed in no more than one sentence. You may notice that you have more than one self-defeating thought about the trigger. But for now, stick to just one. Later, you'll learn how to handle the multiple self-defeating thoughts that come with most triggers.

Step 4

Self-Empowering Thought: Now on the line immediately below the self-defeating thought, talk yourself out of your self-defeating belief. In doing this, you can use one or more strategies, including questions, logic, reasoning, arguments, evidence, facts, statistics, lists, examples, and comparisons. You can also use humor, stories, metaphors, slogans, quotes, and anything else you can think of to put the lie to your self-defeating thought. Finish off your argument with a powerful, one-sentence statement that counters the self-defeating thought.

Step 5

Self-Defeating Behavior: List the self-defeating behaviors that resulted or are likely to result from your self-defeating thoughts and emotions.

Step 6

Self-Empowering Behavior: Identify and record the self-empowering behaviors that you will use to replace the self-defeating behaviors from step 5.

Six-Step Reframe Example

Feeling: Excited.

Trigger: It's Friday night, and my old drinking buddies invited me out to a club to hear a blues band.

Self-Defeating Thought: It would be really fun to go out and have a couple of beers and listen to some tunes with my old buddies.

Self-Empowering Thought: It might start out fun, but in the end, it would be a horror show. After the first drink, I'd feel extremely remorseful for having blown my sobriety. But I'd keep drinking anyway. As usual, I'd overdo it and make an ass of myself. Then I'd black out, get in a fight, smash up my car, or get arrested. How do I know? I know because that's what I've done every time I drank for the last three years. My drinking has progressed to a state where it's unquestionably out of control! How much more evidence do I need? *I can't drink safely!!!* The jig is up. It's over. If I decide to drink tonight, it will be to get wasted. There is no "only a couple of beers" for me—only another bender that will lead me to jail or worse. No thanks, I'm not interested.

Self-Defeating Behavior: Go out with my old drinking buddies, and tie one on. Wake up hungover. Sleep half the day. Blow off my son. Drink to relieve my hangover. Feel like crap. Struggle to get back on the wagon.

Self-Empowering Behavior: Skip the club. Go to an AA meeting with my new sober friends. Then go out and socialize after the meeting. Wake up tomorrow and go for a run. Spend the afternoon with my son. Go out to dinner and a movie with my girlfriend tomorrow night.

Eight-Step Reframe Instructions

Step 1

Feeling: Take out your reframe journal. On the first line, record your emotion or emotions.

Step 2

Trigger: On the second line, identify and record the conditions (i.e., circumstance, person, situation, or event) that triggered your emotional reaction. Be brief and objective when describing the trigger. Record only what actually happened, not your opinion about what happened. Stick to the facts.

Step 3

Self-Defeating Thought: Now is the time to record your opinion about what happened. What is your story? What are you telling yourself about the trigger? It should be expressed in no more than one sentence. You may notice that you have more than one self-defeating thought about the trigger. But for now, stick to just one. Later, you'll learn how to handle the multiple self-defeating thoughts that come with most triggers.

Step 4

Self-Empowering Thought: Now on the line immediately below the self-defeating thought, talk yourself out of your self-defeating belief. In doing this, you can use one or more strategies, including questions, logic, reasoning, arguments, evidence, facts, statistics, lists, examples, and comparisons.

You can also use humor, stories, metaphors, slogans, quotes, and anything else you can think of to put the lie to your self-defeating thought. Finish off your argument with a powerful, one-sentence statement that counters the self-defeating thought.

Step 5

Self-Defeating Behavior: List the self-defeating behaviors that resulted or are likely to result from your self-defeating thoughts and emotions.

Step 6

Self-Empowering Behavior: Identify and record the self-empowering behaviors that you will use to replace the self-defeating behaviors from step 5.

Step 7

Mental Imagery Rehearsal: Get into a comfortable position. Relax your mind and body. Imagine yourself successfully carrying out the self-empowering behaviors from step 6. Mentally rehearse how you want to act. You may also imagine the destructive and harmful consequences of engaging in the self-defeating behaviors from step 5. This will help you associate the pain of indulging in self-defeating behaviors, making it less likely that you will do it again.

Step 8

New Feeling: Record the emotion or emotions you are feeling now that you've completed the reframe.

Eight-Step Reframe Example

Feeling: Excited.

Trigger: It's Friday night, and my old drinking buddies invited me out to a club to hear a blues band.

Self-Defeating Thought: It would be really fun to go out and have a couple of beers and listen to some tunes with my old buddies.

Self-Empowering Thought: It might start out fun, but in the end, it would be a horror show. After the first drink, I'd feel extremely remorseful for having blown my sobriety. But I'd keep drinking anyway. As usual, I'd overdo it and make an ass of myself. Then I'd black out, get in a fight, smash up my car, or get arrested. How do I know? I know because that's what I've done every time I drank for the last three years. My drinking has progressed to a state where it's unquestionably out of control! How much more evidence do I need? *I can't drink safely!!!* The jig is up. It's over. If I decide to drink tonight, it will be to get wasted. There is no "only a couple of beers" for me—only another bender that will lead me to jail or worse. No thanks, I'm not interested.

Self-Defeating Behavior: Go out with my old drinking buddies, and tie one on. Wake up hungover. Sleep half the day. Blow off my son. Drink to relieve my hangover. Feel like crap. Struggle to get back on the wagon.

Self-Empowering Behavior: Skip the club. Go to an AA meeting with my new sober friends. Then go out and socialize after the meeting. Wake up tomorrow and go for a run. Spend the afternoon with my son. Go out to dinner and a movie with my girlfriend tomorrow night.

Mental Imagery Rehearsal: I imagine myself telling my old drinking buddies I won't be able to go out with them, and I thank them for thinking of me. I see myself sitting in an AA meeting surrounded by a room full of my new sober friends and acquaintances. No one's drinking. No one's drunk—especially not me! It feels great being there in my imagination. I flash forward to the next day, imagining myself playing catch with my son and then later that day sitting and talking with my girlfriend.

New Feeling: Relieved, content, honorable.

10-Step Reframe Instructions

Step 1

Feeling: Take out your reframe journal. On the first line, record your emotion or emotions.

Step 2

Trigger: On the second line, identify and record the conditions (i.e., circumstance, person, situation, or event) that triggered your emotional reaction. Be brief and objective when describing the trigger. Record only what actually happened, not your opinion about what happened. Stick to the facts.

Step 3

Self-Defeating Thought: Now is the time to record your opinion about what happened. What is your story? What are you telling yourself about the trigger? It should be expressed in no more than one sentence. You may notice that you have more than one self-defeating thought about the trigger. But for now, stick to just one. Later, you'll learn how to handle the multiple self-defeating thoughts that come with most triggers.

Step 4

Self-Empowering Thought: Now on the line immediately below the self-defeating thought, talk yourself out of your self-defeating belief. In doing this, you can use one or more strategies, including questions, logic, reasoning, arguments, evidence, facts, statistics, lists, examples, and comparisons. You can also use humor, stories, metaphors, slogans, quotes, and anything else you can think of to put the lie to your self-defeating thought. Finish off your argument with a powerful, one-sentence statement that counters the self-defeating thought.

Step 5

Self-Defeating Behavior: List the self-defeating behaviors that resulted or are likely to result from your self-defeating thoughts and emotions.

Step 6

Self-Empowering Behavior: Identify and record the self-empowering behaviors that you will use to replace the self-defeating behaviors from step 5.

Step 7

Mental Imagery Rehearsal: Get into a comfortable position. Relax your mind and body. Imagine yourself successfully carrying out the self-empowering behaviors from step 6. Mentally rehearse the way you want to act. You may also imagine the destructive and harmful consequences of engaging in the self-defeating behaviors from step 5. This will help you associate the pain of indulging in self-defeating behaviors, making it less likely that you will do it again.

Step 8

New Feeling: Record the emotion or emotions you are feeling now that you've completed the reframe.

Step 9

Application: On a lined 3×5 index card, write the qualities, objectives, slogans, techniques, tactics, tools, or other methods you will use to help yourself stay on track. Carry the card with you and read it frequently throughout the day. Apply it to the situations that threaten to hijack your sobriety or peace of mind.

Step 10

Outcome: Use this section to record any observations or information about the situation after some time has passed. Did the thing you were afraid would happen actually happen? Over time you'll notice that most of what you worry about doesn't happen. When it does, it's not as bad as you feared it would be, and you managed to survive or even thrive despite or even because of it. At other times, things turn out far better than you predicted they would. You didn't get fired. You got promoted. The economy didn't collapse. It improved. In using this section, you can also note any mistakes you made and what you plan to do differently next time you find yourself in a similar situation. Use this section to gauge your progress and garner valuable lessons. (See the following example for more help with these instructions.)

10-Step Reframe Example

Feeling: Excited.

Trigger: It's Friday night, and my old drinking buddies invited me out to a club to hear a blues band.

Self-Defeating Thought: It would be really fun to go out and have a couple of beers and listen to some tunes with my old buddies.

Self-Empowering Thought: It might start out fun, but in the end, it would be a horror show. After the first drink, I'd feel extremely remorseful for having blown my sobriety. But I'd keep drinking anyway. As usual, I'd overdo it and make an ass of myself. Then I'd black out, get in a fight, smash up my car, or get arrested. How do I know? I know because that's what I've done every time I drank for the last three years. My drinking has progressed to a state where it's unquestionably out of control! How much more evidence do I need? *I can't drink safely!!!* The jig is up. It's over. If I decide to drink tonight, it will be to get wasted. There is no "just a couple of beers" for me—only another bender that will lead me to jail or worse. No thanks, I'm not interested.

Self-Defeating Behavior: Go out with my old drinking buddies, and tie one on. Wake up hungover. Sleep half the day. Blow off my son. Drink to relieve my hangover. Feel like crap. Struggle to get back on the wagon.

Self-Empowering Behavior: Skip the club. Go to an AA meeting with my new sober friends. Then go out and socialize after the meeting. Wake up tomorrow and go for a run. Spend the afternoon with my son. Go out to dinner and a movie with my girlfriend tomorrow night.

Mental Imagery Rehearsal: I imagine myself telling my old drinking buddies I won't be able to go out with them, and I thank them for thinking of me. I see myself sitting in an AA meeting surrounded by a room full of my new sober friends and acquaintances. No one's drinking. No one's drunk—especially not me! It feels great being there in my imagination. I flash forward to the next day, imagining myself playing catch with my son and then later that day sitting and talking with my girlfriend.

New Feeling: Relieved, content, honorable.

Application: The man takes a drink. The drink takes a drink. The drink takes the man.

Outcome: I skipped going to the club and went to an AA meeting with my new sober friends instead. We went out and socialized after the meeting. I woke up feeling great the next day and went for a run, which made me feel even better. I spent the afternoon with my son. We had a great time shooting hoops. Later that night, I went out to dinner and a movie with my girlfriend. I love being sober!

Extended Reframe Example

The previous instructions and examples allowed for only one self-defeating thought per trigger. In reality, most (if not all) triggers come with multiple self-defeating thoughts. Depending on how much time you have, identify and dispute as many self-defeating thoughts as you can. Here is an example of an extended reframe, covering multiple self-defeating thoughts:

Feeling: Excited.

Trigger: It's Friday night, and my old drinking buddies invited me out to go to a club to hear a blues band.

Self-Defeating Thought: It would be fun to go out and have a couple of beers and listen to some tunes with my old buddies.

Self-Empowering Thought: It might start out fun, but in the end, it would be a horror show. After the first drink, I'd feel extremely remorseful for having blown my sobriety. But I'd keep drinking anyway. As usual, I'd overdo it and make an ass of myself. Then I'd black out, get in a fight, smash up my car, or get arrested, then thrown in jail. How do I know? I know because that's what I've done every time I've had a "couple" of beers for the past six months. My drinking has progressed to a stage where it's out of control. How much more evidence do I need? *I can't drink safely!!!* The jig is up. It's over, finished, complete. If I decide to drink tonight, it will be to get wasted. There is no "couple of beers" for me—only another bender that will lead me to jail or worse. No thanks, I'm not interested.

Self-Defeating Thought: I'll drink just this one more time.

Self-Empowering Thought: If I choose to drink tonight, I'll most certainly end up drinking tomorrow, and the day after that, and for weeks, months, or maybe even years to come until I hit another hellish bottom. What's the point in drinking one more time? I've already done it "one more time" a hundred times. I know where it leads, and I don't want to go there again. It's not worth it. Just as there is no chance of me drinking a couple of beers, there's no chance of me drinking one more time. Do I get that? I'd better get it. Because if I don't, I can kiss my job, my wife, and my kids goodbye.

Self-Defeating Thought: It's too hard to stop drinking.

Self-Empowering Thought: It may be hard to stop drinking, but it's not too hard. "Too hard" means it can't be done. It means it's not even possible. But if that were true, no one would ever get sober. And of course, people do get sober. While getting sober may be difficult, it's not too difficult. It's only as difficult as it is, no more difficult than that. Getting and staying sober is possible. Others have done it and so can I.

Self-Defeating Thought: I can't stand feeling deprived like this.

Self-Empowering Thought: I know it seems that way, but the truth is, I can stand it. I may not like it. It may be unpleasant. But I can definitely stand it. It's possible to stand any kind of discomfort or pain I'm feeling as long as I'm alive. In fact, there have been times in the past when I couldn't drink, and I stood it. If all the booze in the world were somehow taken away forever, I'd tolerate it. And I'd survive it. I can stand feeling deprived, even though I may not like it.

Self-Defeating Thought: I need immediate gratification. I have no choice. I have to drink.

Self-Empowering Thought: I never need what I want. I only want it. And no matter how much I want it, I still don't need it. I may have what feels like an overwhelming desire to drink, but I still don't have to. I have a choice. I can choose not to drink, even when I have the urge. I can think it through and remind myself that I really don't want to drink. I know what comes after the initial buzz. I'll black out, do something crazy, and wake up hungover. Then I'll drink some more and do something else crazy until I end up in the hospital or in jail. No thanks, I'm not interested. I don't need immediate gratification. I have a choice. And I never have to drink again!

Self-Defeating Behavior: Go out with my old drinking buddies, and tie one on. Wake up hungover. Sleep half the day. Blow off my son. Drink to relieve my hangover. Feel like crap. Struggle to get back on the wagon.

Self-Empowering Behavior: Skip the club. Go to an AA meeting with my new sober friends. Then go out and socialize after the meeting. Wake up tomorrow and go for a run. Spend the afternoon with my son. Go out to dinner and a movie with my girlfriend tomorrow night.

Mental Imagery Rehearsal: I imagine myself telling my old drinking buddies I won't be able to go out with them, and I thank them for thinking of me. I see myself sitting in an AA meeting surrounded by a room full of my new sober friends and acquaintances. No one's drinking. No one's drunk—especially not me! It feels great being there in my imagination. I flash forward to the next day, imagining myself playing catch with my son and then later that day sitting and talking with my girlfriend.

New Feeling: Relieved, content, satisfied.

Application: The man takes a drink. The drink takes a drink. The drink takes the man.

Outcome: I skipped going to the club and went to an AA meeting with my new sober friends instead. We went out and socialized after the meeting. I woke up feeling great the next day and went for a run, which made me feel even better. I spent the afternoon with my son. We had a great time shooting hoops. Later that night, I went out to dinner and a movie with my girlfriend. I love being sober!

Related Thoughts

It's not just thinking about the vice itself that leads us to relapse, though our thoughts generate cravings, and those cravings motivate us to indulge. Yet other thoughts unrelated to vice generate disturbing emotions like anger, anxiety, sadness, and loneliness. When that happens, we indulge to alleviate those painful emotions.

For example, you might find yourself thinking, "It sucks that I recently got divorced, retired from a career I loved, and now I've become even more isolated because of the pandemic." But it's not being divorced, retired, or isolated that upsets you. While those events got the ball rolling, it's what came next that primarily caused you to feel sad and lonely, and that was your interpretation of those events. You feel sad and lonely not because you got divorced, retired, and became isolated but because your brain registered those events as threats to your survival and well-being and flooded your system with the stress hormone cortisol. Then your mind kicked in and interpreted those events and feelings as unfavorable and perhaps even dangerous.

Here's the kicker: You told yourself that being divorced, retired, and isolated is a bad thing, and you believed it. Of course, that's nonsense. Many people love being divorced, retired, and isolated. Some look forward to it. They can't wait to get there. How you judge a situation is what causes you to feel good or bad about it.

True, it's not just your interpretation of being divorced, retired, and isolated. After all, we are social creatures hardwired to be with others, so your brain interprets your isolation as a threat to your survival. That alone makes for unpleasant feelings. Before you even had time to think about it, your brain registered this social isolation as dangerous, even life threatening. Still, it's not an actual threat to your survival. It just feels that way. Your brain got it wrong, and your mind went along for the ride. To get yourself out of this foul mood, you have to rewire your brain. In other words, you have to retrain your brain, using your mind to do it. How specifically will you do that? You guessed it: reframing.

Now that you've read and understand the reframe instructions, there's only one thing left for you to do. No, make that two: start reframing and keep reframing.

In the next chapter, I'll show you how to set up a schedule that includes a daily reframe practice.

Read on.

TAKING IT TO THE STREETS

Knowing is not enough; we must apply.
Willing is not enough; we must do.
—Attributed to Johann Wolfgang von Goethe, writer

In this chapter, we tackle the all-important topic of taking action. If you can't get yourself to act on your good intentions, if you can't get yourself off the couch and onto the playing field, every bit of knowledge and skill you've acquired will be for naught. So let's make sure you don't fall victim to the someday maybe syndrome we examined earlier. We'll start by introducing you to the fundamental action strategy, which will serve as the foundation of all that you think and do. In this way, you'll gain control, thinking only the thoughts you want to think and performing only the behaviors you want to perform.

The Fundamental Action Strategy

The fundamental action strategy expands our original two-step strategy to four steps, from abandon and develop to what you'll come to know and love as the fundamental action strategy. Don't be fooled by its simplicity. It's simple, yes, but not easy. And it's the key to not only living vice-free but to living a life characterized by success and happiness. Follow the basic tenets of the fundamental action strategy, and you'll learn to enjoy your life without resorting to vices of any sort. Print it out and hang it up where you can see it and refer to it every day, so you remember what makes life worth living.

It looks like this:

The Fundamental Action Strategy

- Stop thinking and behaving unskillfully.
- Start thinking and behaving skillfully.
- Continue thinking and behaving skillfully.
- Increase your capacity to think and behave skillfully.

As you can see, the fundamental action strategy is, well, fundamental. Again, I implore you, don't be fooled by its simplicity. As you go through life, you want to build on each of its four directives, making it the foundation of everything you think, feel, say, and do.

Look at each step carefully. Is this what you're doing? Are you following these four directives? Yes? No? Ask yourself, "In what way have I been thinking and behaving skillfully or unskillfully? Where specifically have I started to think and behave more skillfully?" Are you continuing to do so? If you are, great. But are you also increasing your capacity? As you go through your day, aim at getting better at what you do, always striving to improve your performance and sharpen your skills. Think carefully about all four fundamental strategies and learn to recognize when you are and when you aren't following through on these directives. Then get busy following them.

Follow the first of these four strategies, and you'll be living vice-free. Follow the rest, and you'll be living the advancing life. In other words, you'll be steadily making progress toward living your best life and becoming your best self. Make sense? Now, let's see how to do it. We'll start by looking at the role that developing good habits plays in getting and keeping us on course.

What Is a Habit?

A habit is a behavior or a series of behaviors that are performed automatically and routinely. We don't necessarily decide to perform a habit. The decision was made by or for us sometime in the past, often without our being aware of it. The more often the behavior is repeated, the more reflexive and habitual it becomes.

For example, we wake up, reach for the phone, and check the weather. We do it the same way every morning, no decision necessary. We then get out of bed, head to the bathroom, and relieve our bladder—all without giving it a thought. In fact, we're almost certainly thinking about something else while we perform this type of routine behavior. The same goes for getting dressed, fixing and eating breakfast, loading the dishwasher, driving to work, and so on. Habits are performed subconsciously and require little or no effort, so there's little to no drain on our willpower.

As I'm writing this paragraph, I'm chomping on a mouthful of lentils. I can't for the life of me remember shoveling them into my mouth. I did it automatically and unconsciously. When I write and eat at the same time, I'm rarely if ever aware that I'm eating, let alone that I'm typing. I'm so engrossed in what I'm writing that I don't notice. I'm thinking about the content of what I'm writing, but I'm not thinking about how I'm hitting the letters on the keyboard. The typing happens unconsciously.

When I first learned to type, I had to pay attention to striking the keys on the keyboard. Now that typing has become a habit, I no longer need to think about it. One part of my mind does the typing while another part does the thinking, creating, and deciding. My hands type automatically as if they had a mind of their own, while I create the content. Even that sometimes happens automatically, and I think, "Where on earth did that idea come from?"

Habits, then, are behaviors etched into our brains, so we don't have to think about how to perform them. You can drive to work while listening to the news or talking with a passenger sitting next to you, while sipping coffee, eating a donut, or smoking a cigarette. If something jumps out in front of your car, you'll slam on the brakes without giving it a thought. You drive on automatic pilot.

The good news is that your ability to develop and perform habitual actions prevents decision fatigue. Imagine if you had to decide moment to moment the tasks to perform throughout your day, relearning and re-thinking how to do each one. It would be exhausting, to say the least. But although habits save energy, if your habits are mostly bad ones, the energy saved is being spent on self-sabotaging activities that will ultimately lead to your downfall. Fortunately, you can prevent that by developing and performing better habits.

We all routinely engage in both physical and mental habits, so it's im-portant to develop both action-based and thought-based habits. Keeping a reframe journal ensures that you do that. Also, because we are largely creatures of habit, the quality of our lives depends largely on the quality of our habits. This chapter focuses on showing you how to develop the habits that will give you the best chance of realizing the success and happiness you naturally desire.

Habit Stacking

For the most part, human beings run on habit. Our lives are dictated by the habits we've created with the help of our environment and the peo-ple in it. This is a good thing when the habits we've developed are good ones. But for many of us, we've developed at least a few more bad habits than good ones—and for some of us, many more bad ones than good. Developing good habits, lots of good habits, is what we'll be up to in the coming sections of this chapter, starting with learning and adopting the habit of stacking habits.

What is habit stacking, and how does it work?

Habit stacking is the process of choosing and establishing good habits, one on top of another. A good way to do that is to start with your morning routine. What time do you get up in the morning? What time do you want to get up? Decide what that is, and if it's not happening, you're ready to build your first new habit.

Here's how:

Choose the time you want to get up. Set your alarm. If you're currently in the habit of hitting the snooze button, then you have to break that habit and replace it with a new one. What can you do instead of hitting the snooze alarm? You guessed it: Put the alarm on the opposite side of the room, so you have to get out of bed and walk across the room to shut it off. Once you've turned off the alarm, head directly to the bathroom—no going back to bed. Repeat until jumping out of bed instead of hitting the snooze button has become your first new habit.

What's next? You're now getting up on time every morning. You've made it a habit, and you're committed to it. It's time to stack your second habit, which might be taking a shower and getting dressed for work. But let's assume you're already doing that. Now you decide you want to start running in the morning before you take your shower and get dressed for work. Your blood pressure has crept up, and your doctor wants you to lose some weight. You've just identified habit number two. After jumping out of bed and going to the bathroom, you'll throw on your sweatpants and sneakers and go for a run. You now officially have a stack—two new habits: getting up on time and going for a run every morning.

Okay, what's next? Let's say you're currently eating a suboptimal breakfast. You might be skipping breakfast and drinking coffee on the ride to work. When you get to work, you get another cup of coffee, grab some pastries, and wolf them down as you check your emails—not a good habit. What can you do instead? Eat a healthy breakfast at home before you go to work. That's habit number three. And so it goes, one new habit after another, until your days are filled with healthy new habits.

Until you've fully developed a habit that is in fact routine, carrying it out will take effort, and your inner addict will try to sabotage you. Why? Because it prefers the old way of doing things. It likes hitting the snooze button. Forming a new habit initially takes effort, and your inner addict isn't interested in exerting effort. It would rather coast along. We're creatures of habit, remember? Our brains evolved to be efficient. This is sometimes experienced as laziness. To get around this natural tendency to avoid doing the things we don't always feel like doing, we take up the fine art of habit stacking.

The beauty of habit stacking is that it's relatively easy. We start by developing one simple behavior that we can perform without much effort. When the part of our brain that evolved to conserve energy, to be efficient and economical, sees that we're taking on a new or different activity, it will resist. That's why it's important to start with small habits that are easy to perform. They won't elicit much resistance from the part of us that thinks what we're doing now is just fine.

The idea of habit stacking is to start small and work up gradually. If we take on something new that's too difficult, we're asking for trouble.

Once you've performed the new behavior, you need to keep doing it until it becomes second nature, all but effortless. When that happens, you're the owner of a new habit. But wait, you're not done yet. It's time to start establishing your next new habit. As a savvy habit stacker, you'll always be working on new habits, one after another. We call this living the advancing life.

To get started, it's helpful to brainstorm a list of good habits, keeping in mind where they might fit in with your daily routine. If you don't yet have a routine, we'll address that shortly. But you can go ahead and start identifying habits you'd like to establish. Once you've prioritized the items on your list, it's time to start establishing that first new habit.

Let's say your first habit is getting out of bed when your alarm goes off instead of hitting snooze. Once that first habit is established, you'll go to your list, pick the next item, and start working on that. Habit stacking begins with brainstorming a list of potential habits, then arranging the list in the order you'll take them on. The list will never be complete. You'll continue to add to it as time goes by and as you discover new habits you want to establish. Trust me. You can always come up with more. There's no shortage of positive activities that can be turned into good habits.

Good habits will become a part of your routine. For example, let's say you haven't been very successful at keeping your apartment clean because you already have a lot on your plate. Keeping your apartment clean seems impossible. There's so much to do. One way to solve that problem is to break it down into manageable chunks. Dust on Mondays. Wash the floors on Tuesdays. Clean the stove on Wednesdays. If that's too much, spread it out even more. Dust one room Monday, another Tuesday, and another Wednesday, for example. Clean the stovetop one day, and the oven on another. You make keeping your house clean a habit by doing a little every day in an order that makes it easy to remember and perform.

If necessary, create a daily list. Or you may want to create a list for the month with one small task each day. Pick a routine that works for you. Start it and stay with it until keeping a clean apartment becomes a habit. What does all this have to do with living a vice-free life, you ask? Simple. Living in a clean and organized environment makes you feel good. And the better you feel, the less likely you are to relapse.

Your Daily Mindful Routine

If this is your second time through the book—after having read it once to get the gist—you're now working with the 10 steps, the addiction busters, and your reframe journal to identify and eliminate your self-limiting thoughts and behaviors. You're on your way. Congratulations. You've started a journey that is challenging you to go beyond what you once thought possible: to get and remain vice-free and become your best self.

This process includes experiencing and ultimately embracing the unpleasant feelings that come with the challenge of resisting temptation, ditching your bad habits, and replacing them with empowering alternatives. You'll come to accept those feelings as evidence that you're moving beyond your comfort zone. You'll be willing to face them instead of running to your vices. Your journey toward a vice-free life requires mindfully (and sometimes reluctantly) confronting your unpleasant feelings and learning what they have to teach you, which, as you will see, is considerable.

As a serious quitter, you've made the uprooting of your unwholesome habits, vices, addictions, and attachments, along with the suffering that comes with them, the single most important thing in your life. Until you've uprooted these provocateurs, nothing good—or at least, very little good—is possible. And so, you've set a new course for yourself to become not only a serious quitter but also a successful quitter. It's time to get serious about being serious.

In this section, we'll show you how to do that with the help of a daily mindful routine. To help you get and stay on course, it's important to have and follow a daily routine, including a printed schedule that lists the tasks you're committed to undertaking throughout your day. Creating and following a schedule is essential to achieving your vice-free goal.

Create and Follow a Schedule

Our daily lives typically have structure. Many of us divide our days into four main parts: before work, during work, after work, and bedtime. The first part of the day looks something like this: We wake up, take a shower, get dressed, and eat breakfast. Maybe we feed the cat or dog. Maybe we read or watch the news while eating breakfast. Maybe we chat with our spouse and kids. Maybe we help get the kids off to school. Finally, we get in the car and drive to work, listening to more news on the way. This is part one of our day, getting ourselves ready for and off to work.

The second part of our day consists of working. We have a job. We get paid to do it. It puts food on the table. We spend eight or more hours of our day working and commuting to and from work. If we're lucky, we have a career that is interesting and rewarding. It could be work we'd do even if we weren't getting paid. Regardless, most of us have to work—except, of course, if you're a full-time alcoholic or drug addict who doesn't have a job. If that's you, your job starts with a daily routine dedicated to getting sober and finding a job.

The third part of our day consists of activities like changing out of our work clothes and decompressing. Perhaps we turn on the TV and watch the news or a game show to unwind. We eat supper, which might include dessert. Maybe we wash the dishes or load the dishwasher. After supper, we watch more TV. Maybe we have a second helping of dessert or a glass of wine. Some of us smoke a joint, put on headphones, and listen to some tunes. We might watch YouTube or check Facebook or other social media sites. Soon enough, it's time to go to bed. Many of us have a TV in our bedrooms, and we watch a little (or a lot) more TV before falling asleep.

As bad as this is, it's still not the worst-case scenario. But you get the picture. Many of us fill our days with what turn out to be little more than distractions. Our days are made up of mindless activities, including listening to the radio, watching TV, surfing the web, hanging out on social media sites, watching sports, or playing video games.

It's not the structure that's a problem. It's the content. While you probably won't need to change the current structure of your day (although some of you will), you will want to change what that structure contains. Structuring your day, in this case, means filling its four sections with as many recovery-related tasks as possible, along with other self-empowering activities. Developing a daily mindful routine is a powerful way to do that. To get started on developing good habits, create and follow a daily mindful routine.

Type it, print it, place it where you can see it, and most important, follow it! Develop the habit of looking at your schedule before and after each task. Even though I perform the same tasks in virtually the same order six days a week, I take a moment to look at my schedule before and after each task. I find it grounding and rewarding. It reminds me that what I'm doing, what I've done, and what I'll be doing next are important. It reminds me where I've been, where I am, and where I'll go next. It's hard to feel lost when you have a daily schedule that you consult and follow this way.

Because I'm currently self-employed and living debt-free with a sufficient income, I get to set my schedule in any way I please. I understand this is not the case for everyone. You may have a job that takes up a good chunk of your day. If you currently have a job and a spouse and children who want your attention, you may assume your time for training is limited.

This is never the case.

Our approach is to take what life gives us, whatever that is, and work with it, turning it to our advantage. That's your real job—applying the *Breakaway Recovery* strategies and tools to whatever comes your way. Your spouse and children are part of the training. The work you're doing to support them is part of the training. Life, all of it, in whatever form it takes, is your training! It's hard to go wrong when you take this approach.

Whatever your circumstances, create a schedule in as much detail as makes sense, listing as many training tasks as you can fit into it. This will include scheduling time to review the various sections of this book, especially the addiction chain, 10 steps of *Breakaway Recovery*, prelapse and relapse questions, and addiction busters. Most of all, be sure to schedule time to reframe. Then keep at it until you become and remain vice-free.

Once you've become vice-free, you'll no longer need the 10 steps or the addiction busters. But you'll continue to follow a daily mindful routine, all the while using your reframe journal as you work at becoming your best self. It's also crucial that you read and study the books listed in appendix A. If you want to become the best version of yourself, becoming an unapologetic self-help junkie is par for the course.

Remember, life is an ongoing journey to becoming your best self. Reading this book is only the first step in bringing you to the domain where your best self is waiting to be discovered. Along with reading this book and others listed in appendix A, make it your business to find and work with top-notch teachers, mentors, and coaches, along with taking the best workshops, seminars, trainings, and retreats.

Should you decide this is who you want to be, you're committing to a lifelong process of gaining insights and achieving breakthroughs, transformations, and self-actualization. Becoming vice-free is but the first stage of this journey, with many more to come. Those of us who have been introduced to these possibilities are extremely fortunate. Let us never forget that as we travel this path. We are privileged indeed. Let's remain worthy of that privilege.

But I digress. Back to the daily schedule.

I arrange my daily mindful routine as a series of tasks (a to-do list, if you will), using a four-part structure similar to the structure of before work, during work, after work, and sleep. I label my four parts morning, afternoon, evening, and lights out.

My morning, afternoon, and evening to-do lists are spot on. They include only the tasks that are in line with my values and goals. I perform them virtually every day, six days a week, in the order they appear on the list. Here's what it looks like:

Daily Mindful Routine

Reality permitting (I add this to remind myself that conditions beyond my control will sometimes interrupt my routine, and that's okay.)

Morning To-Do List

Meditate

Declaration

Pedal, HIIT, binder

First meal

Write

Check email

Afternoon To-Do List

Second meal

Write

Reframe

Meditate

Client meetings

Tasks, chores, and errands

Bike ride

Evening To-Do List

Day in review

Gratitude list

Meditate

Read

YouTube

Dharma talk

Lights Out

Sleep

If you have a job that takes up the second part of your day, your to-do list will include work, and it may take up a big part of your day. Do your best to squeeze in some reading and especially a reframe, no matter what! If you have a full-time job, your schedule might look something like this:

Daily Mindful Routine
Reality permitting

Before Work
Wake up
Meditate
Review yesterday's reframe
Run
Shower
Eat breakfast

Work
Commute to work
Read daily sayings book
Perform work-related tasks
Eat lunch
Reframe
Perform work-related tasks
Commute home

After Work
Eat dinner
Help kids with homework
Hang with spouse or partner
Day in review (including reframe)
Gratitude list
Meditate
Read

Sleep

If you have a family and a full-time job, it can be challenging to schedule time for reframing, reading recovery-related and self-development literature, meditating, and any other self-development tasks you intend to perform all or most days of the week. Still, it can be done smoothly and seamlessly over time. Start your workday by reading a daily saying from one of your favorite daily sayings books. (See appendix A.) At work, use your morning and afternoon breaks and your lunch hour to write or review a reframe. It's also highly advisable to start a meditation practice. (Check out appendixes A and B for what I consider the best meditation guides.)

Along with reframing and meditating, which are formal practices you perform separately from your job or family responsibilities, there are also practices to perform while you're engaged in your other responsibilities. It is to those on-the-spot practices we turn to now.

The Real-Time Technique

I teach all my counseling and coaching clients the real-time technique, which is a staple of the training. It's essential to both getting and remaining vice-free and for living a centered and advancing life once you've eliminated your vices.

It looks like this:

Real-Time Technique for Addiction

Remember what you're doing as you're doing it.
Recognize when you become distracted.
Respond skillfully to the distraction.
Return to the task at hand.

That's the real-time technique in brief. The second step is "Recognize when you become distracted." Use it for distractions that aren't of an addictive nature. When you're dealing with a temptation to indulge in a vice, recognize that you've been triggered, not merely distracted.

Remember, use this technique for distractions of any sort, but for our purposes, especially for distractions of the addictive nature that tempt you to indulge in a vice.

Step 1

Remember what you're doing as you're doing it.

With your awareness up and running, focus your attention on the task at hand. Pay close attention to what you are doing as you are doing it while staying aware of what's happening within and around you. Remember, awareness knows what's happening in the periphery, including what you're thinking (internal) and what's happening (external).

Step 2

Recognize when you become distracted (triggered).

As you go about your day, remain alert for triggers. At some point, you'll notice that you've been triggered. The trigger could be in your head, such as a thought, memory, or fantasy. Or it could be a physical sense, like a sight, sound, smell, taste, or tactile sensation. This is the vice trying to tempt you and hijack your agenda. Recognize it for what it is: an invitation to throw away your life.

Step 3

Respond skillfully to the distraction (trigger).

Once you recognize that you've been triggered, which may or may not include a craving, you'll counter it with a prepared trigger slogan. Use this to neutralize the trigger and drive out any thoughts you have about indulging. Repeat your trigger slogan as many times as it takes to neutralize the trigger and remove any cravings you experience.

Whenever I encounter a trigger, even if I'm not feeling triggered or have a craving, I repeat my trigger slogan: "I am ET. I train like Bruce Lee. I remain vice-free. I write, and I speak for a fee. That's me." ET stands for Extreme Tom, the person I'm determined to be. Bruce Lee is my training role model. Remaining vice-free is my goal. Writing and speaking is my profession and my passion. It's how I deliver the message of vice-free living and living the advancing life. Delivering that message is my life's mission and something I care deeply about and enjoy immensely.

My trigger slogan is only slightly tongue-in-cheek. I wanted to have fun with it, and I advise you to do the same. Addiction can be a grim business, so making recovery as enjoyable as possible helps to offset that. Have some fun when creating and using your trigger slogan. And when applying it, don't merely parrot your trigger slogan, but think about what it means and apply its meaning to the trigger you're facing.

Step 4

Return to the task at hand.

Once the cravings subside and the occasion for indulging passes, congratulate yourself for not indulging in the addictive behavior, and refocus your attention on the task at hand. Take a moment to appreciate the fact that you're no longer controlled by the vice that triggered you. Then continue engaging wholeheartedly in the task at hand.

Early Rapid Reinterpretation

Early rapid reinterpretation is the relentless, moment-to-moment practice of identifying and eliminating the enemies of your hard-won, vice-free success and happiness. It's at the heart of the real-time technique.

It means applying one or more of the *Breakaway Recovery* strategies, tactics, tools, or techniques to each temptation as it arises in real time. It means letting no trigger go unrecognized. It means letting nothing addiction-related go unchallenged. In this way, you will eliminate the entire range of your addictive thoughts, fantasies, feelings, and behaviors, replacing them with empowering alternatives and simultaneously turning your addictive nature to your advantage.

Did you get that last bit?

You'll be turning the tables on your addictive nature and the vices that have held you hostage for so long. You'll take advantage of your addictive tendencies by harnessing your urges and cravings and putting them to good use. We addicts are an obsessive bunch and can turn this to our advantage. Early rapid reinterpretation helps us do that in real time whenever we are hit with temptation. In this way, triggers, urges, and cravings become our recovery partners. How cool is that?

Slogans

Another on-the-spot technique is the use of slogans. Each of the following slogans contains a mini philosophy. Whenever a trigger hits or some other problem arises, counter your unskillful reactions with a slogan. Find the right slogan for the situation. Not every slogan will resonate.

The Power Slogans

Be the message.

Arrive happy.

Lighten up.

Have fun.

Keep it in the day.

Reduce it down.

Seize the moment.

Stay focused.

Apply the training.

Reframe unceasingly.

Stop playing small.

Get radical.

Be unreasonable.

Defy the odds.

Never say never.

Can do.

Watch me.

Show them.

Kick ass.

Crush it.

Give me that thing.
> (Use when presented with a seemingly impossible task.)

Expect the unexpected.

Shit happens.

Things fall apart.

Let it burst.
> (I once heard that Albert Einstein said this when told he needed an operation for an aneurysm.)

It is what it is.

Fear no adversity.

This is nothing.

It's just another event.	This, too, is the training.
Take what you get.	Trust the process.
There's nothing wrong.	The way out is through.
It's all grist.	This too shall pass.
No exceptions.	Turn it over.
Be glad this happened.	Let it go.
What an opportunity.	Be done with it.

The Magic Word

One more on-the-spot technique is called the magic word. I'll give you four examples. You can, of course, come up with others.

Maybe

Perhaps you're familiar with the "Maybe" story. As you may recall, it's a story about a poor farmer who owns a horse that he hopes he'll be able to breed someday when he gets a second horse. He also has a son, whom he loves dearly. One day, when the son finished cleaning the horse's stall, he opened the gate to leave, and the horse ran out and got away.

Soon the poor farmer's neighbors heard the news and came to comfort him. "We're so sorry to hear about your loss," they said. "That's such a shame."

To which the farmer replied, "Maybe."

The next day, the horse made a surprising return to the farmer's land. The gate to the stall was open, and the horse entered. But that's not all. He had brought along another beautiful horse, and the two horses stood there in the stall, eating hay. The farmer's son saw this surprising turn of events and quickly closed the gate. The farmer was now the happy owner of two beautiful horses, one male and the other female, as it turned out. Now he could breed them and make a good living.

When the neighbors caught wind of the good news, they came by to congratulate the farmer. "We're so happy for you," they said. "What a stroke of good luck."

The farmer replied, "Maybe."

A few days later, the farmer's son was thrown off the wild horse and broke his leg. Again, the neighbors heard the news and came by to console the poor farmer. "We're so sorry to hear about your son's broken leg. How unfortunate."

To which the farmer again replied, "Maybe."

A few days later, military officers showed up at the farmer's door to draft his son into the military. When they saw the boy and his broken leg, they concluded he was unfit for battle. When the neighbors heard this news, they came by and said, "Wow! It turns out the broken leg was a blessing in disguise. How fortunate you are."

The farmer replied, "Maybe."

Every time you find yourself confronted with what appears to be an unfortunate event, say the magic word "maybe." Remind yourself of the farmer's story and that what looks like a stroke of bad luck may turn out to be a blessing in disguise. There's almost always a way to turn adversity to our advantage, and the "Maybe" story reminds us that life often does the job for us. It also reminds us to avoid getting attached (i.e., addicted) to your interpretations and expectations of what happens, bad or good.

How fortunate. Well, maybe.

Irrelevant

The ancient Stoic philosophers instructed their students to be aware of the difference between what was within their control and what wasn't. They were taught to steer clear of judging as either good or bad that which was beyond their control. What was uncontrollable was irrelevant, they learned. Finally, the students were told to remain indifferent to what was irrelevant, attending instead to what was relevant—the things they could control and their response to the things they couldn't.[19]

---

19   Epictetus, *Discourses,* 1.11; 2.22; 3.24.

And so it is with us. If we have an ounce of sense, we'll stop trying to control the uncontrollable and focus instead on the things we can control. If you catch yourself feeling depressed about the fact that you're turning 70, for instance, say to yourself, "Irrelevant." Then turn your attention to something over which you do have control. Turning a year older is beyond your control, so it's neither good nor bad. Because it's neither good nor bad, it's irrelevant. Because it's irrelevant, there's no point in thinking about it, certainly not in worrying about it. Accept it, then let it go and get busy living.

Make this your new habit. If need be, take a minute to think it through until you prove to yourself that whatever you can't control is indeed irrelevant and that you're wasting precious time dwelling on it. We know what's beyond our control, so often saying "irrelevant" and promptly letting it go will do the trick. And once you've developed the habit, you'll become a person who rarely if ever dwells on or struggles with the uncontrollable and clearly knows the difference between what's relevant and what's not. It's all part of the new you!

One more thought—if the magic word "irrelevant" isn't working for a particular problem, take out your reframe journal as soon as you have time. Some problems require more than one of the on-the-spot techniques. A written reframe or multiple reframes over time is often required to snuff out a stubborn negative thought pattern or habit.

Perfect

When something is beyond your control, you can't change it, but you can change how you respond to it. And you can respond to it in a way that leaves you better off than you were before the event or situation arose. You can turn the situation to your advantage by using it as a perfect training opportunity to study, practice, or apply one or more of the *Breakaway Recovery* strategies.

The next time you're confronted with a set of conditions you can't change or control, ask yourself how you can use it as a training opportunity. Then say to yourself, "Perfect!" It may be perfect in any number of ways, but certainly it's perfect as a reframe opportunity. If you think about it, everything is perfect just as it is. We just have to learn how to see it as perfect. As the philosopher and naturalist Henry David Thoreau put it, "There [is] as much comfort in perfect disease as in perfect health, the mind always conforming to the condition of the body."[20] Apparently, Thoreau was even able to view illness (he was dying of tuberculosis at the time) as perfect.

Conform to the conditions you can't change, accepting them as they are and using them as a perfect training opportunity. Perfect!

Somehow

When I began college in my early 30s, I found myself struggling to keep up. I lacked a basic understanding of the subjects I was studying because I had spent most of my previous time in school staring out the window or skipping classes altogether. I was pushed through the public school system without learning even the basics of history, math, English, or any other subject. I lamented to my therapist that I might have to drop out, but my therapist assured me I could do it. I argued that it was impossible. Once again, she insisted I could.

I became adamant and raised my voice, asking, "How? *How?* HOW?"

In her usual relaxed manner, my therapist replied, "Somehow."

That one word stopped me in my tracks. Somehow. I'll do it somehow. I didn't have to know how right then, but all I had to do was keep trying, and I'd figure out how. And figure it out I did. I found a deck of flash cards and a tutor at the college's Learning Center, and I went at it like the good little addict that I am. I went at it like a dope fiend chasing his next fix.

Now, whenever I think I can't do something and find myself asking, "How? How on earth will I do this?" I answer, "Somehow." And before long, the "how" reveals itself, and I get busy doing the thing I thought I couldn't do. And so will you. How? Somehow!

---

20   F. B. Sanborn, *Henry D. Thoreau*, rev. ed., (Boston, MA: Houghton Mifflin & Company, 1882), 310–311.

Embark

Google's Oxford Languages dictionary tells us that to "embark" is "to begin (a course of action, especially one that is important or demanding)."[21] For those of you who have read through *Breakaway Recovery* once, you are now ready to embark on the most important journey of your life. It's time to go back and start performing the exercises. It's time to take each of the 10 steps of *Breakaway Recovery*. Go back to chapter 3, reread the instructions, and follow them, applying them to your addictive triggers and cravings. It's time to start using your reframe journal and create your daily mindful routine. Congratulations, you're on your way to the adventure of a lifetime!

Ready, Set, Go!

For those of you who have read through the book twice, you are now in possession of everything you need to get and remain vice-free. This book contains it all. Study it daily. Make it your constant companion, keeping it with you wherever you go and consulting it frequently throughout the day. Spend most of your leisure time reading and rereading this book. But most of all, spend your time applying what you learn. Read and *follow* the instructions.

Know that there is a science to eliminating addictive behaviors, and it is a precise and reliable science, much like arithmetic and geometry. There are discernible laws that govern the process of becoming and remaining vice-free. Once you understand and follow these laws, you will become vice-free with mathematical certainty. The steps spelled out in this book are based on those laws. Getting sober and becoming vice-free comes from following these steps.

I wish you the best in your journey to recovery. But you don't need my wishes, only your own study, practice, and application of the material presented here. Godspeed.

---

21 Oxford Languages, s.v. "embark," accessed February 5, 2024, https://www.google.com/search?q=embark+definition.

Up, Up, and Away!

Before we go, I'd like you to meet someone. He's one of my first clients as an addictions counselor and the first to latch on to the tools you've been introduced to in this book.

At the tender age of nine, Steve (not his real name) took his first drink. Earlier that fateful night, while his mother was in her bedroom passed out from drinking, Steve was in the kitchen playing with matches. As fate would have it, he ended up burning his fingers and was in serious pain. But because his mother had schizophrenia and was such a mean drunk, he was afraid to wake her to ask for help.

Instead, his older brother snuck into her room and came out with a bottle of her Scotch whisky. He handed it to Steve, telling him it would ease his pain. And ease his pain it did—not just his physical pain but also the gnawing emotional pain that had been Steve's constant companion for as long as he could remember. That moment of emotional release set the wheel of addiction in motion.

His older brother, who tried his best to be supportive of his younger brother, was already mainlining heroin at the time. Steve's father had run off with another woman years earlier.

After the match incident, Steve didn't drink again until he was 12. On that occasion, Steve's friend's father drove him and his two buddies up to a cabin in Vermont for the weekend and bought them some beer on the way. They all got drunk and did impulsive things they later regretted. The experience of that weekend helped Steve refrain from getting drunk for another three years. Seeing his brother addicted to drugs also helped dissuade him from drinking.

In the summer of 1970, Steve drank again with two buddies on the rooftop of their 19-story apartment building. The only things he remembers were getting drunk and singing the Schaefer beer jingle while standing on the edge of the roof, peeing off the side.

For his sophomore year in high school, Steve was sent to a boarding school in Maine. On his arrival, he almost immediately started smoking weed, drinking alcohol, and taking various pills, including barbiturates and LSD every weekend. His grades were good in the beginning but gradually went downhill as his substance abuse increased. Still, he had good SAT scores and decent enough grades to get into college as a math major. He quickly decided to switch majors to social science because he couldn't combine weed and drink and pass the math course requirements.

Steve dropped out after one year and bummed around Massachusetts, drinking and partying with his girlfriend. They married and had two children, but Steve and his wife spent most of their time together drinking and eventually decided to get divorced. Soon after, Steve took his first shot at sobriety with AA. He was 24 years old and managed to remain sober for five years.

During that time, Steve started a business as a disc jockey and was able to pay his way through college where he got mostly As. Then he went to a psychiatrist for help with panic attacks and was prescribed Xanax, which initially seemed like a miracle drug. But it wasn't long before he started abusing the medication. It was his senior year in college, and things went downhill fast after that.

Steve made several unsuccessful attempts to stay sober. Around this time, he married his second wife, whom he met at a Narcotics Anonymous (NA) meeting. Steve's panic attacks, along with his alcohol and drug use, continued to escalate. Over the next seven years, he bounced in and out of treatment programs, including detoxes and long-term stays, and eventually checked into the dual diagnosis ward at Leonard Morse Hospital. Steve then divorced his second wife and quickly married his third wife, whom he met at AA. Steve's panic attacks continued to torment him, so he went to see another psychiatrist and got prescriptions for Xanax, Valium, and Klonopin. Of course, he ended up mixing them with alcohol and weed. This led to his third marriage ending in divorce.

Steve was eventually committed to the addiction unit inside Bridgewater State Penitentiary for a 30-day stay. That scared him sober for another year, while he remained on five different psych meds. By this point, Steve had been declared disabled. He lived in a rooming house for a while but wound up in a shelter.

He felt hopeless. He knew if he stayed on Ativan, he was doomed to a life of addiction and homelessness. But without it, his panic attacks and anxiety would be unbearable. He briefly considered taking his life but decided to try treatment one more time. He had heard of an addiction treatment center and called daily for two weeks until they finally said he could come in for an intake assessment. During the intake, they agreed to help him get off the Ativan, and the plan was for him to be admitted to their nine-month residential program once he detoxed off the Ativan.

By this time, Steve had been in and out of AA and NA meetings, treatment programs, shelters, and state institutions for decades. He was not only a chronic drug user but also a chronic relapser. No matter how many times he got up, he always fell back down. But likewise, no matter how many times he fell down, he always got back up. Still, he wasn't at all optimistic that this stay would be any different.

Once off the Ativan, Steve was admitted to the residential program. He was still taking an antidepressant, a mood stabilizer, an antipsychotic, and a blood pressure medication. On his second day there, Steve was assigned a morning job and went to his first class after lunch.

He entered the classroom and took a seat among hardened drug addicts, many with criminal records. He felt anxious, depressed, and utterly hopeless because he knew from years of experience that AA wasn't going to work. Therapy wasn't going to work. Medication wasn't going to work, including the medication he was still taking, and programs, including this one, weren't going to work.

The instructor walked into the room, and everyone quieted down. The instructor was me.

"Good morning," I said. "My name is Tom."

"Hi, Tom," everyone enthusiastically replied in unison. This greeting, at the beginning of each group, was a program tradition.

I went on, "If anyone sitting here is struggling with getting and staying sober, if you have a long history of relapsing, if you've tried AA, NA, therapy, other programs, or anything else, and none of it has worked, if you're feeling anxious, depressed, and hopeless, I want you to know there is a solution you haven't yet tried because no one has introduced you to it. But I'll be introducing you to that solution in the days to come."

Steve's ears perked up.

"Somehow, the way you said it, the tone in your voice, the look on your face, your obvious conviction in what you were saying gave me a glimmer of hope," he told me later. "I thought I had tried everything. You name it, I tried it. But there you were saying you had something different, something I hadn't tried. I sat there, glued to my chair, anticipating what you would say next."

I then turned to the whiteboard behind me and wrote this:

EXPERIENCE CHAIN
Trigger
Thought
Emotions
Behavior
Outcome

I explained, "This deceptively simple formula sums up our lives. 'Trigger' represents the people, places, and things we encounter. 'Thought' is what we tell ourselves about them, our interpretations of what we encounter. 'Emotion' is how we feel about those interpretations. 'Behavior' is what we do. And 'outcome' is the result of our behavior."

I went on to explain reframing and finished by saying that anyone who was interested could visit me during my office hours to get handouts, books, and individual help.

I was new on the job at the time, and this was one of the first classes I'd taught, so I was excited to see someone respond the way Steve did. He became the first member of what would become the Deadly Dogs, a self-selected group who took their recovery seriously. They showed up at my office hours to get handouts, borrow books, and get individual instruction in reframing, meditation, and other related skills.

Steve was also the first to learn and practice the 10-step reframing process I had developed. I remember one of his roommates commenting that every morning like clockwork he'd wake up and see Steve sitting up in bed, writing in his journal. Steve was faithfully doing his daily reframe followed by a half hour of meditation.

I eventually started a reframe group. During the morning meeting, I announced that at 1:00 p.m. every weekday, I'd be up in the conference room on the second floor, and anyone interested in learning to reframe was welcome to come. It was strictly voluntary. The group always fluctuated, with between 10 and 20 of the 75 residents showing up. Some came and listened, and a few brought and read their reframes for feedback. Steve always had multiple reframes to read and offered helpful feedback and inspiration.

During Steve's nine-month stay, his panic attacks stopped. Then he slowly weened his way off the psych meds. Steve came to realize it was his own thinking and behavior that was the problem, not some alleged chemical imbalance in his brain. Steve learned to take charge of his thinking and his behavior, and that made all the difference.

It's been 28 years since Steve graduated from the residential treatment program, and he remains drug- and alcohol-free. Three years after graduating, he met his current wife. They've been together for 25 years and happily married for nine with three houses, two in Massachusetts and one in Florida. He currently works as the director of information technology and the facilities manager for a large financial investment firm.

Breakaway Recovery transformed the life of a seemingly hopeless alcohol and drug addict. Once depressed, panic stricken, unemployable, and unhoused, Steve committed to using this strategy to end his addictive behaviors and start his path to personal happiness and professional success.

What might *Breakaway Recovery* do for you?

RECOMMENDED READING

Addiction

The Urge: Our History of Addiction by Carl Erik Fisher

Unbroken Brain: A Revolutionary New Way of Understanding Addiction by Maia Szalavitz

Psychiatry

Anatomy of an Epidemic: Magic Bullets, Psychiatric Drugs, and the Astonishing Rise of Mental Illness in America by Robert Whitaker

Mind Fixers: Psychiatry's Troubled Search for the Biology of Mental Illness by Anne Harrington

Reframe

Feeling Right When Things Go Wrong by Bill Borcherdt

How to Stubbornly Refuse to Make Yourself Miserable About Anything, Yes Anything! by Albert Ellis, PhD (Especially see "Appendix 2: How to Maintain and Enhance Your Rational Emotive Behavior Therapy Gains")

How to Make Yourself Happy and Remarkably Less Disturbable by Albert Ellis, PhD

How to Control Your Anxiety Before it Controls You by Albert Ellis, PhD

Meditation and Buddhism

The Mind Illuminated: A Complete Meditation Guide Integrating Buddhist Wisdom and Brain Science by Culadasa (John Yates, PhD), Matthew Immergut, PhD, with Jeremy Graves

Mindfulness: A Practical Guide to Awakening by Joseph Goldstein

Mindfulness with Breathing: A Manual for Serious Beginners by Buddhadasa Bhikkhu, translated by Santikaro Bhikkhu

Pure and Simple: The Extraordinary Teachings of a Thai Buddhist Laywoman by Upasika Kee Nanayon, translated by Thanissaro Bhikkhu

Meditation on Perception: Ten Healing Practices to Cultivate Mindfulness by Bhante Gunaratana

Beyond Distraction: Five Practical Ways to Focus the Mind by Shaila Catherine

Heartwood of the Bodhi Tree: The Buddha's Teachings on Voidness by Buddhadasa Bhikkhu

Under the Bodhi Tree: Buddha's Original Vision of Dependent Co-arising by Buddhadasa Bhikkhu

The Buddha Before Buddhism: Wisdom from Early Teachings by Gil Fronsdal

Noble Truth, Noble Path: The Heart Essence of the Buddha's Original Teachings (The Teachings of the Buddha) by Bhikkhu Bodi

The Magnanimous Heart: Compassion and Love, Loss and Grief, Joy and Liberation by Narayan Helen Liebenson

The Science of Enlightenment: How Meditation Works by Shinzen Young

Evolutionary Psychology and Neuroscience

Habits of a Happy Brain: Retrain Your Brain to Boost Your Serotonin, Dopamine, Oxytocin, and Endorphin Levels by Loretta Graziano Breuning, PhD

Status Games: Why We Play and How to Stop by Loretta Graziano Breuning, PhD

Stoic Philosophy

Stoicism and the Art of Happiness: Practical Wisdom for Everyday Life by Donald Robertson

Stress Management

Six Seconds to True Calm: Thriving Skills for 21ˢᵗ Century Living by Robert
Simon Siegel, MS

Chronic Pain

Break Through Pain by Shinzen Young
*You Are Not Your Pain? Using Mindfulness to Relieve Pain, Reduce Stress, and
Restore Well-Being* by Vidyamala Burch and Danny Penman

The Philosophy of Idealism

*Why Materialism Is Baloney: How True Skeptics Know There Is No Death
and Fathom Answers to Life, the Universe, and Everything* by Bernardo
Kastrup
*The Idea of the World: A Multi-Disciplinary Argument for the Mental Nature
of Reality* by Bernardo Kastrup

Daily Sayings

Daily Wisdom: 365 Buddhist Inspirations by Joshua Bartok (editor)
*The Daily Stoic: 366 Meditations on Wisdom, Perseverance, and the Art of
Living* by Ryan Holiday
365 Tao: Daily Meditations by Deng Ming Dao
Above & Beyond: 365 Meditations for Transcending Chronic Pain and Illness
by J.S. Dorian

MEDITATION INSTRUCTIONS

Some of you may be thinking, "Why the meditation instructions? What does meditation have to do with recovery?" Plenty! Remember, essential to overcoming addiction is a well-trained mind. While reframing trains you to think and behave skillfully, meditation trains you to be aware and to pay attention. It teaches you to recognize, examine, and let go of your addictive thoughts and cravings; *and* it teaches you to *focus* and *stay* focused on living your best life.

Beware, however, your addiction can always come up with a list of reasonable-sounding excuses why you should give in to temptation. Being skilled in reframing *and* meditation empowers you to catch and reject those excuses and temptations before they get the best of you; and that's just the beginning of what these two powerhouses will do for you.

For those of you with little or no experience in Buddhist meditation, you'll need additional help with the meditation instructions, especially 7 through 28, help that is beyond the scope of this book. You will get that help by reading the books in the "Meditation and Buddhism" section of appendix A. These books will answer your questions and clarify what you'll need to know to follow meditation instructions 7 through 28. They will prepare you to try some of these more advanced exercises.

Some of you may not be interested in Buddhist teachings to that degree. Still, you can benefit greatly from the first six meditation instructions.

If you learn and practice just these first six instructions, you'll be doing yourself a great service in terms of your recovery, no Buddhist philosophy or psychology needed.

While Buddhism itself isn't for everyone, I would argue that virtually everyone *can* benefit from a meditation practice. The first six meditation instructions below will bring you those benefits.

Meditation Practice Setup

Establish a relaxed, comfortable, upright, and stable sitting position. Take a few minutes to get in a position you can maintain with as little tension and discomfort as possible. Put aside any concerns you have regarding your other responsibilities and interests.

Resolve to stay *focused* on the task at hand.

During each of the following tasks, maintain peripheral awareness while simultaneously focusing your attention on the chosen target. See how *closely*, how *precisely*, how *exclusively* you can focus your attention, zeroing in on the chosen target as it presents itself in real time, all the while distinguishing between awareness and attention. *Really try!*

Whenever you suddenly realize your attention has wandered off the target, be grateful for this realization. Always take a moment to appreciate these aha moments whenever they occur. Then redirect your attention back to the chosen target, reengaging *wholeheartedly* in the task at hand. *Really try!*

Be *relentless* in redirecting your attention back to the chosen target over and over, again and again, as often as necessary, with no objections, no annoyance, and no sense of exasperation. There's nothing wrong. This is the process:

- Direct the attention.
- Sustain the attention.
- Become distracted.
- Forget the meditation target.

- Become lost in thought.
- Suddenly realize you've become lost in thought.
- Be grateful for this sudden realization.
- Redirect your attention back to the chosen target.
- Engage wholeheartedly with the chosen target.

Be more than happy to repeat this process over and over, again and again for the duration of your meditation sessions. By the end of task 7, you'll seldom get lost in thought, you'll recognize it sooner when you do, and you'll get better at staying with the breath sensations for longer stretches of time.

Meditation Instructions 1: Be Present

Goals

Establish and maintain present-moment awareness with free, roaming attention.

Instructions

Open your awareness to the present moment, aware of the context you find yourself occupying, knowing where you are and what's happening around, on, and within your body. Tune in to the here and now.

With your awareness alert and open to whatever presents itself, let your attention roam freely among the auditory and tactile sensations arising and passing away, moment by moment in the here and now. Pay close attention to the sounds and sensations that present themselves one after another. When thoughts arise, allow them to remain in the background of your awareness, giving all your attention to the auditory and tactile sensations that capture your attention.

Allow your attention to linger on any sound or tactile sensation it feels drawn to while remaining aware of the context you find yourself occupying. Distinguish between awareness and attention, letting the attention roam and linger as it will.

The Real-Time Technique

Remember what you're doing as you're doing it.
Recognize that you've become distracted.
Respond skillfully to the distraction.
Return to the task at hand.

Meditation Instructions 2: Relax the Body Sitting

Goals

Establish and maintain deep physical relaxation throughout the body as you sit. See how loose and relaxed the body can get.

Step 1

Direct your attention to the body sitting. As you breathe in, notice any tightness, tension, or strain associated with the body sitting.

Step 2

When the lungs are comfortably full and the body signals that it's time, breathe out. As you breathe out, relax and let go. Feel any tightness, tension, or strain associated with the body being released as you breathe out smoothly and comfortably.

Step 3

After exhaling, rest as comfortably as you can without breathing in for as long as you comfortably can. Relax the entire body as deeply as you can, enjoying yourself as much as you can until the body signals that it's time to breathe in again.

Step 4

When the body signals that it's time to breathe in, go back to step 1 and start the process again. Relax a little deeper with each breath. Let the body become softer and more relaxed each time you breathe out. Continue in this way for as long as you like. The more you practice, the better you'll get at relaxing the body sitting.

The Real-Time Technique

Remember what you're doing as you're doing it.

Recognize that you've become distracted.

Respond skillfully to the distraction.

Return to the task at hand.

Meditation Instructions 3: Relax the Body Breathing

Goals

Establish and maintain deep relaxation of all breathing-related activities. See how relaxed the breathing can get.

Step 1

Direct your attention to the body as you breathe in. Feel the lungs expand as the body breathes in. Recognize any tightness, tension, or strain associated with the body breathing in.

Step 2

When the lungs are comfortably full and the body signals that it's time, breathe out. Relax and let go as the body breathes out, relaxing all breathing-related muscles and activities as deeply as you can. Let the breathing become loose, relaxed, and at ease.

Step 3

After exhaling, rest as comfortably as you can without breathing in for as long as you comfortably can, further relaxing all breathing-related muscles and activities as deeply as you can, enjoying yourself as much as you can until the body signals that it's time to breathe in again.

Step 4

When the body signals that it's time to breathe in, go back to step 1 and start the process again. Relax the breathing a little more each time you exhale. Let the breathing become more and more relaxed with each out-breath. Continue practicing in this way for as many breaths as you like. The more you practice, the better you'll get at relaxing the body breathing.

The Real-Time Technique

Remember what you're doing as you're doing it.

Recognize that you've become distracted.

Respond skillfully to the distraction.

Return to the task at hand.

Meditation Instructions 4: Passively Allow Breathing

Goals

Establish and maintain a powerful, nonintrusive mindfulness of breathing. See how nonintrusive you can be.

Step 1

Direct your attention to the body breathing in. Breathe in naturally and automatically without trying to control or alter the breathing in any way. Passively experience the body breathing in, allowing it to happen naturally and automatically in its own way and at its own rate. Don't try to pull the breath in quickly, and don't try to slow it down.

Step 2

When the in-breath is complete and the body signals that it's time, breathe out naturally and automatically without trying to control or alter the breathing in any way. Passively experience the body breathing out in its own way and at its own rate. Don't try to push the breath out quickly, and don't try to slow it down.

Step 3

After exhaling, remain mindful of the pause that occurs naturally between the out-breath and the in-breath. Let the body pause naturally and automatically without trying to control or alter the pause in any way. Passively experience the body pausing in its own way and at its own rate. Don't try to lengthen the pause, and don't try to shorten it. Just be mindful of the pause with no other agenda of your own until the body signals that it's time to breathe in again.

Step 4

When the body signals that it's time to breathe in, go back to step 1 and start the process again. Continue practicing in this way for as many breaths as you like. The more you practice, the better you'll get at passively experiencing the body breathing naturally and automatically in its own way.

The Real-Time Technique

Remember what you're doing as you're doing it.
Recognize that you've become distracted.
Respond skillfully to the distraction.
Return to the task at hand.

Meditation Instructions 5: Focus the Attention

Goals

Establish and maintain sustained, focused attention on the sensations associated with the breath touching the nostrils. See how focused you can get.

Step 1

Direct your attention to the sensations associated with the breath coming in the body at the nostrils. Focus on the breath sensations in real time, *as they are happening.* Focus your attention *exclusively* on the sensations associated with the breath touching the nostrils for the *full* duration of the in-breath, zeroing in on the breath sensations in this small area of the body.

Step 2

When the body signals that it's time, exhale. Maintain your focus on the breath sensations at the nostrils as you breathe out. Focus on these sensations in real time, *as they are happening.* Focus your attention *exclusively* on the breath sensations at the nostrils for the full duration of the out-breath, zeroing in on the breath sensations in this small area of the body.

Step 3

After exhaling, maintain your focus on the sensations related to the air still touching the nostrils as you sit still, neither breathing in nor out. Sit perfectly still and experience these subtle sensations until the body signals that it's time to breathe in again.

Step 4

When the body signals that it's time to breathe in, go back to step 1 and start the process again. Continue in this way for as many breaths as you like. The more you practice, the better you'll get at sustaining your attention on the breath sensations at the nostrils.

The Real-Time Technique

Remember what you're doing as you're doing it.
Recognize that you've become distracted.
Respond skillfully to the distraction.
Return to the task at hand.

Strategies for Sustained Attention

Task 1

Imagine you are playing basketball. Each time you achieve a complete in-breath and a complete out-breath without being distracted and without losing focus, that counts as a basket. Use the time between breaths to aim your attention at the "basket" in preparation for your next "shot." Take as much time as necessary between shots. See how many baskets you can get. *Really try!*

Task 2

Focus your attention on the breath sensations at the nostrils during each in-breath, each out-breath, and each pause, treating each as a separate, independent, autonomous exercise. During the pause, maintain your focus on the sensations related to the air still touching the nostrils, enjoying these subtle sensations until the body signals that it's time to breathe again. *Really try!*

Task 3

See if you can feel the breath sensations related to the air touching the nostrils *precisely* as they're happening in real time. During the pause, maintain your focus on the sensations related to the air still touching the nostrils, experiencing these barely perceptible sensations *precisely* as they're happening in real time. *Really try!*

Task 4

See if you can discern the very first breath sensation of each in-breath and the very last breath sensation of each out-breath. *Really try!*

Task 5

Discern as many individual breath sensations as possible as you breathe in and again as you breathe out. During the pause, maintain your attention on the breath sensations related to the air touching the nostrils as you sit still, breathing neither in nor out. *Really try!*

Task 6

Think of yourself as following the breath, like following someone in a car. The car in front is leading the way to a destination. You don't want to lose it, or you won't get where you want to go. You must stay right behind it as it drives ahead of you. If the car you're following slows down, you slow down. If it speeds up, you speed up. If it switches lanes, you switch lanes. If it takes an exit, you take the same exit, staying right behind it, always keeping pace with it, never losing sight of it. You don't want to let another car get behind it. You don't want any cars getting between the two of you, so you must stay right on its tail.

Likewise, you want your attention to follow behind the breath sensations as you meditate. Stay with them as your body breathes in and out, never losing touch with them, never letting a distraction get between you and the breath sensations, never letting a distraction take your attention away. Be sure your attention follows the breath sensations as closely as possible for the entire meditation session, all the way to your destination, *samadhi* (profound concentration). *Really try!*

Task 7

As you sit with your attention directed to the breath sensations touching the nostrils, see if you can hold the body perfectly still, preventing even the slightest movements. *Really try!*

Task 8

As you sit with your attention directed to the breath sensations touching the nostrils, see if you can hold the mind perfectly still, preventing any thoughts from arising. *Really try!*

Task 9

While focusing your attention on the breath sensations at the nostrils, see if you can count and stay with each breath all the way up to 10 breaths. If you lose count, start over until you can make it to 10 without losing count. Once you make it to 10, move on to the next task. *Really try!*

Task 10

Challenge yourself to follow as many consecutive breaths as you can, following the entire in-breath, then the entire out-breath, and finally the entire pause, for as many consecutive breaths as possible. See how many consecutive breaths you can follow this way before becoming distracted, forgetting the breath, and becoming lost in thought. Challenge yourself to follow as many consecutive breaths as you can. *Really try!*

Meditation Instructions 6: Sort for Pleasure

Goals

Establish and maintain a pleasant, abiding here and now by eliciting and dwelling in the four *jhanas* (progressively refined states of concentration).

Step 1

Once the attention is sharply focused on the sensations of air moving in and out at the nostrils, shift your attention from the breath sensations to the pleasantness of these sensations. Tune in to just the pure pleasantness of the breath sensations. Ignore everything else. Make the pleasure itself, not the actual breath sensations, the new focus of your attention.

Step 2

Continue in this way for as long as you like. The more you practice, the better you'll get at experiencing the pure pleasure associated with the pleasant breath sensations.

The Real-Time Technique

Remember what you're doing as you're doing it.
Recognize that you've become distracted.
Respond skillfully to the distraction.
Return to the task at hand.

Meditation Instructions 7: Discern Impermanence of the Breath Sensations

Goals

Establish and maintain penetrating insight into the impermanent nature of the breath sensations at the nostrils. See how clearly you can discern the impermanence of these sensations.

Step 1

Tune in to the breath sensations at the nostrils as the body breathes in. Experience the impermanent, ever-changing nature of the breath sensations as the body breathes in.

Step 2

When the in-breath is complete and the body signals that it's time, breathe out. Experience the impermanent, ever-changing nature of the breath sensations as the body breathes out.

Step 3

After exhaling, maintain your focus on the breath sensations related to the air still touching the nostrils as you sit, neither breathing in nor out. Sit perfectly still while you continue to experience the impermanent, ever-changing nature of these subtle breath sensations at the nostrils.

Step 4

When the body signals that it's time to breathe in, go back to step 1 and start the process again. Continue in this way for as many breaths as you like. The more you practice, the better you'll get at discerning the impermanent, ever-changing nature of the breath sensations.

The Real-Time Technique

Remember what you're doing as you're doing it.
Recognize that you've become distracted.
Respond skillfully to the distraction.
Return to the task at hand.

Meditation Instructions 8: Investigate Body-Related *Dukkha*

Goals

Develop penetrating insight into *dukkha* (suffering) and its relationship to the physical discomfort inherent in having a body.

Gain a profound understanding of *dukkha* and its cause.

Step 1

Direct your attention to the scalp. Recognize and experience any discomfort occurring in this area of the body. Examine the relationship between the discomfort in this area and the *dukkha* that accompanies it.

Step 2

Using the same technique, systematically work your way through the body in the following sequence: scalp, forehead, eyeballs, eyelids, cheeks, jaw, mouth, tongue, neck, shoulders, arms, hands, trunk, hips, groin, buttocks, legs, and feet.

Step 3

Continue in this way for as long as you like. The more you practice recognizing, experiencing, and examining the discomfort associated with having a body and the *dukkha* that accompanies it, the more insight you'll gain into *dukkha* and its cause.

The Real-Time Technique

Remember what you're doing as you're doing it.
Recognize that you've become distracted.
Respond skillfully to the distraction.
Return to the task at hand.

Meditation Instructions 9:
Extinguish Body-Related *Dukkha*

Goals

Abide peacefully with the discomfort inherent in having a body. See how peacefully you can coexist with the discomfort associated with having a body.

Step 1

Direct your attention to the physical sensation in the scalp. Recognize and experience any discomfort present in this area of the body.

Step 2

Recognize and experience any aversion, resistance, or cravings related to the discomfort present in this part of the body.

Step 3

Let go of any aversion, resistance, or cravings related to the discomfort present in this part of the body.

Step 4

Systematically work your way through the body in the following sequence: scalp, forehead, eyeballs, eyelids, cheeks, jaw, mouth, tongue, neck, shoulders, arms, hands, trunk, hips, groin, buttocks, legs, and feet. Scan through the body in this way as many times as you like. The more you practice, the better you'll get at abiding peacefully with the discomfort inherent in having a body.

The Real-Time Technique

Remember what you're doing as you're doing it.
Recognize that you've become distracted.
Respond skillfully to the distraction.
Return to the task at hand.

Meditation Instructions 10: Investigate Breathing-Related *Dukkha*

Goals

Develop penetrating insight into *dukkha* and its relationship with the physical discomfort inherent in the process of breathing.

Gain a profound understanding of *dukkha* and its cause.

Step 1

Direct your attention to the body breathing in. Recognize and experience any discomfort and *dukkha* associated with the body breathing in. Examine the relationship between the discomfort of breathing in and the *dukkha* that accompanies it.

Step 2

When the lungs are full and the body signals that it's time, breathe out. Recognize and experience any discomfort and *dukkha* associated with the body breathing out. Examine the relationship between the discomfort of breathing out and the *dukkha* that accompanies it.

Step 3

After exhaling, recognize and experience any discomfort and *dukkha* associated with the pause that occurs naturally between the out-breath and the in-breath. Examine the relationship between the discomfort of pausing and the *dukkha* that accompanies it.

Step 4

Continue practicing in this way for as long as you like. The more you practice recognizing, experiencing, and examining the discomfort and *dukkha* associated with breathing, the more insight you'll gain into *dukkha* and its cause.

The Real-Time Technique

Remember what you're doing as you're doing it.
Recognize that you've become distracted.
Respond skillfully to the distraction.
Return to the task at hand.

Meditation Instructions 11: Extinguish Breathing-Related *Dukkha*

Goals

Abide peacefully with the discomfort associated with the body breathing. See how peacefully you can coexist with the discomfort inherent in the breathing process.

Step 1

Direct your attention to the body breathing in. As the body breathes in, recognize and experience any discomfort associated with breathing in. Let go of any aversion, resistance, or craving related to the discomfort associated with the body breathing in.

Step 2

When the lungs are full and the body signals that it's time, breathe out. As the body breathes out, recognize and experience any discomfort associated with breathing out. Let go of any aversion, resistance, or craving related to the discomfort associated with the body breathing out.

Step 3

After exhaling, recognize and experience any discomfort associated with the pause that naturally occurs between the out-breath and the in-breath. Let go of any aversion, resistance, or craving related to the discomfort associated with the body pausing.

Step 4

When the body signals that it's time to breathe in, go back to step 1 and start the process again. Continue practicing in this way for as long as you like. The more you practice, the better you'll get at abiding peacefully with the discomfort associated with the body breathing.

The Real-Time Technique

Remember what you're doing as you're doing it.
Recognize that you've become distracted.
Respond skillfully to the distraction.
Return to the task at hand.

Meditation Instructions 12: Contemplate the Anatomical Parts

Goals

Establish and maintain powerful mindfulness of the anatomical parts. See how mindful of the anatomical parts you can be.

Gain direct, firsthand, liberating insight into the impermanent, stressful, and selfless nature of the anatomical parts.

Know that the anatomical parts are unworthy of being conceived of as "me" or "mine."

Step 1

Contemplate the body down from the top of the head to the soles of the feet and back up to the top of the head. Enclosed by skin, the body is full of many unclean things. This body is made up of skin, head hair, body hair, nails, teeth, flesh, sinews, muscle, bones, bone marrow, brains, heart, lungs, liver, kidneys, diaphragm, spleen, stomach, stomach contents, intestines, bowels, bladder, urine, feces, bile, phlegm, snot, pus, blood, fat, tears, grease, saliva, and oil of the joints.

Step 2

Experience the arising and passing away of each body part. Contemplate how each body part comes in and out of existence. Contemplate the impermanent, stressful, and selfless nature of the body parts.

Step 3

Continue in this way for as long as you like. The more you practice contemplating the body parts, the better you'll get at recognizing and discerning the impermanent, stressful, and selfless nature of the body.

The Real-Time Technique

Remember what you're doing as you're doing it.
Recognize that you've become distracted.
Respond skillfully to the distraction.
Return to the task at hand.

Meditation Instructions 13: Contemplate the Corpse in Decay

Goals

Establish and maintain powerful mindfulness of the corpse in decay. See how mindful of the corpse in decay you can be.

Gain direct, firsthand, liberating insight into the impermanent, stressful, and selfless nature of the corpse in decay.

Know that the corpse in decay is unworthy of being conceived of as "me" or "mine."

Step 1

Imagine a corpse thrown on the ground out in the open, one to three days dead, swollen, bloated, blue, livid, festering, and oozing fluids. Apply this image to your own body. This body, too, is of the same nature, shares the same fate, and has the same future.

Imagine the corpse being picked at by crows, vultures, hawks, dogs, hyenas, worms, and various other organisms. Apply this image to your own body. Think, this body, too, is of the same nature, shares the same fate, and has the same future. Now imagine the body reduced to a skeleton held together by tendons smeared with blood and pieces of flesh. Apply this image to your own body. Think, this body, too, is of the same nature, shares the same fate, and has the same future. Now imagine a fleshless skeleton smeared with blood. Apply this image to your own body. Think, this body, too, is of the same nature, shares the same fate, and has the same future. Now imagine a skeleton with no flesh, no blood—only bones. Apply this image to your own body. Think, this body, too, is of the same nature, shares the same fate, and has the same future. Now imagine a skeleton broken apart, reduced to bones scattered in all directions, a hand here, a foot there—shin bones, thigh bones, pelvis, vertebrae, and skull all scattered about. Apply this image to your own body. Think, this body, too, is of the same nature, shares the same fate, and has the same future. Now imagine bones bleached white after lying in a pile for more than a year. Apply this image to your own body. Think, this body, too, is of the same nature, shares the same fate, and has the same future.Now imagine bones reduced to powder, crumbled to dust, blown about by the wind. Apply this image to your own body. Think, this body, too, is of the same nature, shares the same fate, and has the same future.

Step 2

Experience the arising and passing away of the corpse in decay. Contemplate how the corpse comes in and out of existence. Contemplate the impermanent, stressful, and selfless nature of the corpse in decay.

Step 3

Continue in this way for as long as you like. The more you practice contemplating the corpse in decay, the better you'll get at recognizing and discerning its impermanent, stressful, and selfless nature.

The Real-Time Technique

Remember what you're doing as you're doing it.
Recognize that you've become distracted.
Respond skillfully to the distraction.
Return to the task at hand.

Meditation Instructions 14: Examine the Four Properties

Goals

Establish and maintain powerful mindfulness of the four properties: solid, liquid, gas, and temperature. See how mindful of these properties you can be.

Gain direct, firsthand, liberating insight into the impermanent, stressful, and selfless nature of these properties.

Know that the four properties are unworthy of being conceived of as "me" or "mine."

Step 1

Tune in to the body. Analyze the body in terms of the four properties. The body has a solid property, liquid property, gas property, and temperature property. Experience the solid property as solid, the liquid property as liquid, the gas property as gas, and the temperature property as temperature.

Step 2

Experience the arising and passing away of each property. Contemplate how each property comes in and out of existence. Contemplate the impermanent, stressful, and selfless nature of four properties.

Step 3

Continue in this way for as long as you like. The more you practice contemplating the four properties, the better you'll get at recognizing and discerning their impermanent, stressful, and selfless nature.

The Real-Time Technique

Remember what you're doing as you're doing it.
Recognize that you've become distracted.
Respond skillfully to the distraction.
Return to the task at hand.

Meditation Instructions 15: Examine the Five Aggregates

Goals

Establish and maintain powerful mindfulness of the five aggregates. See how mindful of the aggregates you can be.

Gain direct, firsthand, liberating insight into the impermanent, stressful, and selfless nature of the five aggregates.

Know that the five aggregates are unworthy of being conceived of as "me" or "mine."

Step 1

Tune in to the mind-body experience. Analyze the mind-body experience in terms of the five aggregates. Know form to be form, sensation to be sensation, perception to be perception, thought to be thought, and consciousness to be consciousness.

Step 2

Experience the arising and passing away of each aggregate. Contemplate how each aggregate comes in and out of existence. Contemplate the impermanent, stressful, and selfless nature of the five aggregates.

Step 3

Continue in this way for as long as you like. The more you practice contemplating the aggregates, the better you'll get at recognizing and discerning their impermanent, stressful, and selfless nature.

The Real-Time Technique

Remember what you're doing as you're doing it.
Recognize that you've become distracted.
Respond skillfully to the distraction.
Return to the task at hand.

Meditation Instructions 16: Experience Feeling Tones

Goals

Establish and maintain powerful mindfulness of the three feeling tones—pleasant, unpleasant, and neutral. See how mindful of these feeling tones you can be.

Gain direct, firsthand, liberating insight into the impermanent, stressful, and selfless nature of the three feeling tones.

Know that the three feeling tones are unworthy of being conceived of as "me" or "mine."

Step 1

Bring your attention to the forehead and be aware of the feeling tones in this area of the body as you allow the breathing to continue naturally and effortlessly in the background. Spend as much time as you like experiencing the feeling tones in this area.

Step 2

Experience the arising and passing away of the feeling tones. Contemplate the impermanent, stressful, and selfless nature of the three feeling tones.

Step 3

Using the same technique, systematically work your way through the body in the following sequence: scalp, forehead, eyeballs, eyelids, cheeks, mouth, jaw, neck, shoulders, arms, hands, trunk, hips, groin, buttocks, legs, and feet.

Step 4

Continue in this way for as long as you like. The more you practice contemplating the three feeling tones, the better you'll get at recognizing and discerning their impermanent, stressful, and selfless nature.

The Real-Time Technique

Remember what you're doing as you're doing it.

Recognize that you've become distracted.

Respond skillfully to the distraction.

Return to the task at hand.

Meditation Instructions 17: Recognize Reactions to Feeling Tones

Goals

Establish and maintain powerful mindfulness of the three reactions—attraction, aversion, and indifference. See how mindful of these reactions you can be.

Gain direct, firsthand, liberating insight into the impermanent, stressful, and selfless nature of the reactions.

Know that the three reactions are unworthy of being conceived of as "me" or "mine."

Step 1

Bring your attention to the forehead and be aware of any feeling tones in this part of the body as you allow the breathing to continue naturally and effortlessly in the background. Identify any reactions in the mind related to the three feeling tones.

Step 2

Using the same technique, systematically work your way through your body in the following sequence: scalp, forehead, eyeballs, eyelids, cheeks, mouth, tongue, jaw, neck, shoulders, arms, hands, trunk, hips, groin, buttocks, legs, and feet.

Step 3

Continue in this way for as long as you like. The more you practice contemplating the three reactions, the better you'll get at recognizing and discerning their impermanent, stressful, and selfless nature.

The Real-Time Technique

Remember what you're doing as you're doing it.
Recognize that you've become distracted.
Respond skillfully to the distraction.
Return to the task at hand.

Meditation Instructions 18: Quiet Reactions to Feeling Tones

Goals

Experience the three feeling tones with detachment and equanimity. See how detached and nonreactive you can be.

Step 1

Tune in to the three feeling tones—pleasant, unpleasant, and neutral—present in the forehead as you allow the breathing to continue naturally and effortlessly in the background. Be aware of the feeling tones without reacting to them. Maintain a serenely detached and nonreactive awareness of whatever feelings you experience. Serenely accept and remain detached from and nonreactive to whatever feelings arise.

Step 2

Using the same technique, systematically work your way through your body in the following sequence: scalp, forehead, eyeballs, eyelids, cheeks, mouth, tongue, jaw, neck, shoulders, arms, hands, trunk, hip, groin, buttocks, legs, and feet.

Step 3

Continue in this way for as long as you like. The more you practice tuning in to the three feeling tones, the better you'll get at experiencing them without reacting.

The Real-Time Technique

Remember what you're doing as you're doing it.
Recognize that you've become distracted.
Respond skillfully to the distraction.
Return to the task at hand.

Meditation Instructions 19: Recognize and Examine the Torments

Goals

Establish and maintain powerful mindfulness of the torments. See how mindful of the torments you can be.

Gain direct, firsthand, liberating insight into the impermanent, stressful, and selfless nature of the torments.

Know that the torments are unworthy of being conceived of as "me" or "mine."

Step 1

Tune in to the mind. Analyze the mind in terms of the torments.

Know when there is craving in the mind. Know when the mind is free from craving.

Know when there is aversion in the mind. Know when the mind is free from aversion.

Know when there is lethargy in the mind. Know when the mind is free from lethargy.

Know when there is restlessness in the mind. Know when the mind is free from restlessness.

Know when there is rumination in the mind. Know when the mind is free from rumination.

Know when there is worry in the mind. Know when the mind is free from worry.

Know when there is doubt in the mind. Know when the mind is free from doubt.

Whatever torments there may be, know if they are present or not.

Step 2

Experience the arising and passing away of each torment. Contemplate the impermanent, stressful, and selfless nature of each torment.

Step 3

Continue in this way for as long as you like. The more you practice contemplating the torments, the better you'll get at recognizing and discerning their impermanent, stressful, and selfless nature.

The Real-Time Technique

Remember what you're doing as you're doing it.
Recognize that you've become distracted.
Respond skillfully to the distraction.
Return to the task at hand.

Meditation Instructions 20: Investigate and Remove the Torments

Goals

Establish and maintain freedom from the torments. See how free from the torments you can be.

Step 1

Tune in to the mind. Know when there is craving in the mind. Know how it has arisen. Know how to remove it. Remove it. Know how to prevent it from returning. Prevent it from returning.

Know when there is aversion in the mind. Know how it has arisen. Know how to remove it. Remove it. Know how to prevent it from returning. Prevent it from returning.

Know when there is lethargy in the mind. Know how it has arisen. Know how to remove it. Remove it. Know how to prevent it from returning. Prevent it from returning.

Know when there is restlessness in the mind. Know how it has arisen. Know how to remove it. Remove it. Know how to prevent it from returning. Prevent it from returning.

Know when there is rumination in the mind. Know how it has arisen. Know how to remove it. Remove it. Know how to prevent it from returning. Prevent it from returning.

Know when there is worry in the mind. Know how it has arisen. Know how to remove it. Remove it. Know how to prevent it from returning. Prevent it from returning.

Know when there is doubt in the mind. Know how it has arisen. Know how to remove it. Remove it. Know how to prevent it from returning. Prevent it from returning.

Whatever torment there may be in the mind, know how it has arisen. Know how to remove it. Remove it. Know how to prevent it from returning. Prevent it from returning.

Step 2

Continue in this way for as long as you like. The more you practice, the better you'll get at removing and preventing the torments.

The Real-Time Technique

Remember what you're doing as you're doing it.
Recognize that you've become distracted.
Respond skillfully to the distraction.
Return to the task at hand.

Meditation Instructions 21: Investigate and Remove the Fetters

Goals

Establish and maintain freedom from the fetters. See how free from the fetters you can be.

Step 1

Tune in to the mind. Know the eyes, the forms, and the fetters that arise dependent on both. Know how the fetters arise and how to remove them. Remove them. Know how to prevent them from arising in the future. Prevent them from arising in the future.

Know the ears, the sounds, and the fetters that arise dependent on both. Know how the fetters arise and how to remove them. Remove them. Know how to prevent them from arising in the future. Prevent them from arising in the future.

Know the nose, the odors, and the fetters that arise dependent on both. Know how the fetters arise and how to remove them. Remove them. Know how to prevent them from arising in the future. Prevent them from arising in the future.

Know the tongue, the flavors, and the fetters that arise dependent on both. Know how the fetters arise and how to remove them. Remove them. Know how to prevent them from arising in the future. Prevent them from arising in the future.

Know the body, the touches, and the fetters that arise dependent on both. Know how the fetters arise and how to remove them. Remove them. Know how to prevent them from arising in the future. Prevent them from arising in the future.

Know the mind, the mind-objects, and the fetters that arise dependent on both. Know how the fetters arise and how to remove them. Remove them. Know how to prevent them from arising in the future. Prevent them from arising in the future.

Step 2

Continue in this way for as long as you like. The more you practice, the better you'll get at removing and preventing the fetters.

The Real-Time Technique

Remember what you're doing as you're doing it.
Recognize that you've become distracted.
Respond skillfully to the distraction.
Return to the task at hand.

Meditation Instructions 22: Experience Fading Away

Goals

Experience the fading away of *dukkha* and the cause of *dukkha*. See how clearly you can detect the fading away of *dukkha* and its cause.

Step 1

As you breathe in, recognize and experience the fading away of *dukkha*. Focus on the fading away of *dukkha* and its cause.

Step 2

As you breathe out, recognize and experience the fading away of *dukkha*. Focus on the fading away of *dukkha* and its cause.

Step 3

As the body pauses between the out-breath and the next in-breath, recognize and experience the fading away of *dukkha*. Focus on the fading away of *dukkha* and its cause.

Step 4

Continue in this way for as long as you like. The more you practice, the better you'll get at recognizing and experiencing the fading away of *dukkha* and its cause.

The Real-Time Technique

Remember what you're doing as you're doing it.
Recognize that you've become distracted.
Respond skillfully to the distraction.
Return to the task at hand.

Meditation Instructions 23: Realize the Cessation of *Dukkha*

Goals

Realize the cessation of *dukkha* and the cause of *dukkha*. See how completely you can realize the cessation of *dukkha* and its cause.

Step 1

As you breathe in, recognize and experience the cessation of *dukkha*. Focus on the cessation of *dukkha* and its cause.

Step 2

As you breathe out, recognize and experience the cessation of *dukkha*. Focus on the cessation of *dukkha* and its cause.

Step 3

As the body pauses between the out-breath and the next in-breath, recognize and experience the cessation of *dukkha*. Focus on the cessation of *dukkha* and its cause.

Step 4

Continue in this way for as long as you like. The more you practice, the better you'll get at recognizing and experiencing the cessation of *dukkha* and its cause.

The Real-Time Technique

Remember what you're doing as you're doing it.
Recognize that you've become distracted.
Respond skillfully to the distraction.
Return to the task at hand.

Meditation Instructions 24: Relinquish All Claims to Me and Mine

Goals

Experience freedom from attachment to self, others, and the world. See how free from these attachments you can be.

Step 1

As you breathe in, let go of all clinging to self, others, and the world. Relinquish your attachments to all claims of me and mine.

Step 2

As you breathe out, let go of all clinging to self, others, and the world. Relinquish your attachments to all claims of me and mine.

Step 3

As the body pauses between the out-breath and the next in-breath, let go of all clinging to self, others, and the world. Relinquish your attachments to all claims of me and mine.

Step 4

Continue in this way for as long as you like. The more you practice, the better you'll get at relinquishing all claims of me and mine.

The Real-Time Technique

Remember what you're doing as you're doing it.
Recognize that you've become distracted.
Respond skillfully to the distraction.
Return to the task at hand.

Meditation Instructions 25: Cultivate the Factors of Awakening

Goals

Establish and maintain the factors of awakening. Cause them to develop and reach full growth and perfection.

Step 1

Tune in to the mind. Know if mindfulness is present or absent. Know how to awaken it. Awaken it. Know how to develop it. Develop it. Know how to bring it to full growth and perfection. Bring it to full growth and perfection.

Know if investigation is present or absent. Know how to awaken it. Awaken it. Know how to develop it. Develop it. Know how to bring it to full growth and perfection. Bring it to full growth and perfection.

Know if energy is present or absent. Know how to awaken it. Awaken it. Know how to develop it. Develop it. Know how to bring it to full growth and perfection. Bring it to full growth and perfection.

Know if joy is present or absent. Know how to awaken it. Awaken it. Know how to develop it. Develop it. Know how to bring it to full growth and perfection. Bring it to full growth and perfection.

Know if tranquility is present or absent. Know how to awaken it. Awaken it. Know how to develop it. Develop it. Know how to bring it to full growth and perfection. Bring it to full growth and perfection.

Know if concentration is present or absent. Know how to awaken it. Awaken it. Know how to develop it. Develop it. Know how to bring it to full growth and perfection. Bring it to full growth and perfection.

Know if equanimity is present or absent. Know how to awaken it. Awaken it. Know how to develop it. Develop it. Know how to bring it to full growth and perfection. Bring it to full growth and perfection.

Step 2

Continue in this way for as long as you like. The more you practice, the better you'll get at engendering the awakening factors and causing them to develop and reach full growth and perfection.

The Real-Time Technique

Remember what you're doing as you're doing it.

Recognize that you've become distracted.

Respond skillfully to the distraction.

Return to the task at hand.

Meditation Instructions 26: Consummate the Four Noble Truths

Goal
Gain direct, firsthand, liberating knowledge of the Four Noble Truths.

Step 1
Understand *dukkha*.

Step 2
Abandon the cause of *dukkha*.

Step 3
Realize the cessation of *dukkha*.

Step 4
Follow the path to the cessation of *dukkha*.

The Real-Time Technique
Remember what you're doing as you're doing it.
Recognize that you've become distracted.
Respond skillfully to the distraction.
Return to the task at hand.

The Fruits of Practice
Knowing all physical and mental phenomena to be impermanent, stressful, and without self, abide independently, not clinging to anything in the world.

Mindfulness Instructions 27: Posture and Activities Setup

Take a few minutes to orient yourself to the present moment. Bring your attention to the body, and resolve to maintain this present-moment orientation in all body postures and activities.

Mindfulness of Postures

Goals

Establish and maintain powerful mindfulness of the body's postures. See how mindful of these postures you can be.

Gain direct, firsthand, liberating insight into the impermanent, stressful, and selfless nature of the body's postures.

Know that the body's postures are unworthy of being conceived of as "me" or "mine."

Step 1

Direct your attention to the body's postures. When standing, know you are standing. When sitting, know you are sitting. When reclining, know you are reclining. When lying down, know you are lying down. However the body is positioned, know it as it is.

Step 2

Experience the arising and passing away of the postures. Contemplate the impermanent, stressful, and selfless nature of the body's postures.

Step 3

Continue in this way for as long as you like. The more you practice contemplating the body's postures, the better you'll get at recognizing and discerning their impermanent, stressful, and selfless nature.

The Real-Time Technique

Remember what you're doing as you're doing it.
Recognize that you've become distracted.
Respond skillfully to the distraction.
Return to the task at hand.

Mindfulness Instructions 28: Mindfulness of Activities

Goals

Establish and maintain powerful mindfulness of the body's activities. See how mindful of these activities you can be.

Gain direct, firsthand, liberating insight into the impermanent, stressful, and selfless nature of the body's activities.

Know that the body's activities are unworthy of being conceived of as "me" or "mine."

Step 1

Direct yourself to the body's activities. When walking forward or returning, know you are walking forward or returning. When bending or extending your arm, know you are bending or extending your arm. When lifting, carrying, or placing an object, know you are lifting, carrying, or placing an object. When drinking, eating, or savoring food, know you are drinking, eating, or savoring food. When urinating or defecating, know you are urinating or defecating. When talking, keeping silent, falling asleep, or waking up, know what you are doing as you are doing it. Whatever you are doing, know that you are doing it as you are doing it.

Step 2

Experience the arising and passing away of each activity. Contemplate the impermanent, stressful, and selfless nature of the body's activities.

Step 3

Continue in this way for as long as you like. The more you practice contemplating the body's activities, the better you'll get at recognizing and discerning their impermanent, stressful, and selfless nature.

The Real-Time Technique

Remember what you're doing as you're doing it.

Recognize that you've become distracted.

Respond skillfully to the distraction.

Return to the task at hand.

Based on *Mahā Satipaṭṭhāna Sutta* (The Great Establishing of Mindfulness Discourse) from the Dīgha Nikāya (The Long Collection or Collection of Long Discourses) translated by Thanissaro Bhikkhu (Metta Forest Monastery, PO Box 1409, Valley Center, CA 92082).

ACKNOWLEDGEMENTS

It would be impossible to list all those who have helped me in one way or another to write this book. Let me start by mentioning my wise and generous siblings who have patiently put up with my shenanigans over these many years and who routinely offer a helping hand whenever one is needed. Thank you Nancy, Paula, George (see, I do know your real name), Billy, and Jennifer. I love you guys.

For the ideas contained in this book I owe much to the late, great Albert Ellis, whose REBT (along with my sister Nancy and her late husband Phil) saved my life when I was at my lowest point. To my Buddhist teachers, to the Stoic Philosophers, and to the countless psychology and philosophy books I've read and reread over the years. I shudder to think where I'd be left to my own devices.

To my Framingham State University professors, especially Bridgette Perry, John Budz, and Barrie Westerman. You taught me so much about psychology and about how to be happy. Thank you, thank you, thank you. I miss you so much.

And finally, to that mysterious force that delivers those unexpected ideas, sentences. and paragraphs just when I need them most. Where they come from remains a mystery.